TOWARDS ZERO

by Agatha Christie and Gerald Verner

samuelfrench.co.uk

ISBN 978-0-573-01455-0

www.samuelfrench.co.uk
www.samuelfrench.com
www.agathachristielimited.com

FOR PRODUCTION ENQUIRIES

UNITED KINGDOM AND WORLD
EXCLUDING NORTH AMERICA
plays@samuelfrench.co.uk
020 7255 4302/01

UNITED STATES AND CANADA
info@SamuelFrench.com
1-866-598-8449

Each title is subject to availability from Samuel French,
depending upon country of performance.

MUSIC USE NOTE

Licensees are solely responsible for obtaining formal written permission from copyright owners to use copyrighted music in the performance of this play and are strongly cautioned to do so. If no such permission is obtained by the licensee, then the licensee must use only original music that the licensee owns and controls. Licensees are solely responsible and liable for all music clearances and shall indemnify the copyright owners of the play(s) and their licensing agent, Samuel French, against any costs, expenses, losses and liabilities arising from the use of music by licensees. Please contact the appropriate music licensing authority in your territory for the rights to any incidental music.

IMPORTANT BILLING AND CREDIT REQUIREMENTS

If you have obtained performance rights to this title, please refer to your licensing agreement for important billing and credit requirements.

TOWARDS ZERO was first presented by Peter Saunders at the St. James's Theatre, London, on September 4, 1956. The performance was directed by Murray MacDonald, with sets by Michael Weight. The cast was as follows:

THOMAS ROYDE................................... Cyril Raymond

KAY STRANGE... Mary Law

MARY ALDIN ....Gillian Lind

MATHEW TREVES .... Frederick Leister

NEVILE STRANGE................................... George Baker

LADY TRESSILIAN...................................Janet Barrow

AUDREY STRANGE.................................Gwen Cherrell

TED LATIMER .... Michael Scott

SUPERINTENDENT BATTLE ....William Kendall

INSPECTOR LEACH.................................Max Brimmell

P.C. BENSON .... Michael Nightingale

CHARACTERS

THOMAS ROYDE
KAY STRANGE
MARY ALDIN
MATHEW TREVES
NEVILE STRANGE
LADY TRESSILIAN
AUDREY STRANGE
TED LATIMER
SUPERINTENDENT BATTLE
INSPECTOR LEACH
P.C. BENSON

SETTING

The action of the play takes place in the drawing room at Gull's Point, Lady Tressilian's house, Saltcreek, Cornwall.

TIME

ACT I

Scene One: A morning in September.
Scene Two: After dinner, four days later.

ACT II

Scene One: Early the following morning.
Scene Two: Two hours later.

ACT III

Scene One: The next morning.
Scene Two: The same evening.

NOTES ON PUBLICATION

Arguably the best known adaptation of Agatha Christie's novel, *Towards Zero*, was that of prolific writer, Gerald Verner, in 1951. However, a few years ago, it was discovered that Agatha Christie had in fact written her own stage adaptation of the novel which was commissioned by the Shuberts in 1944 and we present both plays as part of The Collection.

Both versions of the text follow a similar narrative pattern. The events of both plays explore how the characters, through their various interactions move towards a 'zero hour' of murder. Both explore the idea that murder shouldn't be the beginning of a story but the end.

However, there are some important distinctions between the texts. Christie's adaptation is a three-act, five-scene drama set over eight days with thirteen actors whilst Verner's version is again three acts but with six scenes set over seven days involving eleven actors. Moreover, the setting is different; Christie's is set open air on the terrace of Lady Tressilian's house whereas Verner's takes a more familiar path and is set in the drawing room.

Both plays contain a familiar core group of characters however there are some important roles that differ. Angus McWhirter is perhaps the most important character missing from Verner's text but makes a very significant contribution to Christie's original. His interactions with Audrey are perhaps the most profound of the play – allowing Christie to explore thematically the notions of mortality, suicide, depression and even redemption. In place of McWhirter, Verner employs the shrewd and insightful Mathew Treves, a lawyer who is now house guest and confidant to Lady Tressilian. Verner also uses the well-known and notable Superintendent Battle to lead the murder investigation.

By all accounts Christie's adaptation is a more ambitious and dramatic piece of writing however Verner's play is structurally strong and provides a faithful and well realised adaptation of Christie's original novel.

ACT I

Scene One

(The drawing room at Gull's Point, Lady Tressilian's house at Saltcreek, Cornwall. A morning in September. It is a large, very beautiful room of exquisite taste. French windows open on to a terrace and a further door leads to the other parts of the house. A large bay window shows a view across the river to the Easterhead Bay Hotel. The room is furnished with a sofa and two armchairs, one of which has a standing sewing basket next to it. There is also a coffee table and a bureau bookcase with a framed photograph of Audrey on it. A low butler's tray has been set up with a variety of drinks and glasses. The room stands empty, except for an incongruous carpet sweeper which rests against the wall. **THOMAS ROYDE** *enters immediately by the French windows. He is a good looking, middle-aged man, bronzed by many years in the sun. He carries a suitcase and a set of golf clubs. As he enters, the door leading to the rest of the house bangs shut as if someone had just rushed out.* **ROYDE** *shrugs, then moves to the bay window and stands gazing out.* **KAY STRANGE** *rushes in through the French windows, dressed in tennis kit. Clearly upset, she does not notice* **ROYDE**. *She takes a cigarette from the box on the coffee table then spots the photograph of Audrey. She quickly rips it from the frame,*

7

tears it in half, then discards the pieces in the waste paper basket. **ROYDE** *coughs discreetly.)*

KAY. Oh! Who are you?

ROYDE. I've just walked up from the bus stop. I'm...

KAY. *(Interrupting.)* I know who you are. You're the man from Malaya.

ROYDE. *(Gravely.)* Yes, I'm the man from Malaya.

(There is a pause. **ROYDE** *looks significantly at the waste paper basket.)*

KAY. I just came in to get a cigarette.

*(**KAY** looks at him guiltily. There is an awkward pause.)*

Oh, hell, what's the good of explaining? What do I care what you think, anyway?

(She rushes out through the French windows. **ROYDE** *stares thoughtfully after her.* **MARY ALDIN** *enters busily from the house. She is a dark haired woman of about thirty-six, reserved, pleasant and noncommittal in manner.)*

MARY. Mr. Royde?

*(**ROYDE** holds out his hand.)*

Lady Tressilian is not down yet. I am Mary Aldin, Lady Tressilian's dogsbody.

(They shake.)

ROYDE. Dogsbody?

MARY. The official term is secretary, but as I don't know shorthand – and what talents I do have are purely domestic – "dogsbody" is a much better word.

ROYDE. I know all about you. Lady Tressilian told me in her Christmas letter what a wonderful difference you had made to her.

MARY. I'm very fond of her. She has a lot of personality.

ROYDE. That's quite an understatement. How's her arthritis?

MARY. It makes her rather helpless, poor dear.

ROYDE. I'm sorry about that.

MARY. Can I offer you a drink?

ROYDE. No, thank you.

(He looks out the bay window.)

What's that great caravanserai over there?

MARY. That's the new Easterhead Bay Hotel. It was only finished last year. Isn't it a horror?

(She closes the window.)

Lady Tressilian doesn't like this window opened, she's always afraid that someone might fall out. Yes, Easterhead Bay is a terrific resort, you know, nowadays. I suppose when you came here as a boy there was nothing the other side of the estuary except a few fishermen's cottages.

(She pauses.)

You did come here for your school holiday, didn't you?

ROYDE. Yes, old Sir Mortimer used to take me out sailing, he was mad keen on sailing.

MARY. Yes. He was drowned out there.

ROYDE. Lady Tressilian saw it happen. I wonder she can go on living here.

MARY. I think she preferred to remain with her memories. But she won't have any boat kept here, she even had the boathouse pulled down.

ROYDE. So if I want to sail or go for a row, I've got to go to the ferry?

MARY. Or cross to the Easterhead side. That's where all the boats are nowadays.

ROYDE. I hate changes. Always have. *(Self-consciously.)* May I ask who else is staying here?

MARY. Old Mr. Treves – you know him?

(**ROYDE** *nods.*)

MARY. And the Stranges.

ROYDE. The Stranges? You mean Audrey Strange, Nevile's first wife?

MARY. Audrey, yes. But Nevile Strange and his *new* wife are here, too.

ROYDE. Isn't that a bit odd?

MARY. Lady Tressilian thinks it very odd indeed.

ROYDE. Bit awkward, wot?

> (**MATHEW TREVES** *enters by the French windows. He is an elderly and distinguished lawyer of great experience and shrewdness. He retired from his London firm some years ago and is now a keen observer of human nature.*)

TREVES. Rather too much glare on the terrace today.

> (*He sees* **ROYDE.**)

Ah, Thomas. Nice to see you after all these years.

> (*They shake hands.*)

ROYDE. I'm very glad to be here.

> (**MARY** *looks over Royde's suitcase and golf clubs.*)

MARY. Shall I take your things up to your room?

ROYDE. No, no, I can't let you do that.

> (*He rushes over and picks them up.* **MARY** *nods then leads the way, catching sight of the carpet sweeper as she does so.*)

MARY. (*Vexed.*) Really! Mrs. Barrett! These daily women are impossible. It makes Lady Tressilian very angry when things are left all over the place.

ROYDE. I think my sudden arrival on the terrace frightened the poor woman.

> (*He looks back as* **TREVES,** *who smiles.*)

MARY. Oh, I see.

> (**MARY** *picks up the sweeper and exits into the house.* **ROYDE** *follows.* **TREVES** *quickly notices the empty photo frame then the torn photograph in the waste paper basket. He stoops to pick up the pieces. His eyebrows rise and he makes a little "Tut, tut.")*

KAY. *(Offstage.)* Where are you going to, Nevile?

NEVILE. *(Offstage.)* Only into the house for a moment.

> (**TREVES** *quickly puts the pieces of the photograph back into the waste paper basket.* **NEVILE STRANGE** *enters by the French windows wearing tennis kit.)*

Isn't Audrey here?

TREVES. No.

NEVILE. Where is she? Do you know?

TREVES. I have no idea.

KAY. *(Offstage.)* Nevile – Nevile!

NEVILE. *(Frowning.)* Oh, damn.

KAY. *(Offstage.)* Nevile!

NEVILE. *(Calling.)* Coming – coming.

> (**ROYDE** *enters from the house.)*

ROYDE. Nevile.

NEVILE. Hullo, Thomas.

> *(They shake hands.)*

What time did you get here?

ROYDE. Just now.

NEVILE. Must be quite a long time since I saw you last. When was it you were home, three years ago?

ROYDE. Seven.

NEVILE. Good Lord, is it, really? How time flies.

KAY. *(Offstage.)* Nevile!

NEVILE. *(Calling.)* All right, Kay.

(KAY enters by the French windows.)

KAY. Why can't you come? Ted and I are waiting.

NEVILE. I just came to see if Audrey –

> *(KAY interrupts. She takes NEVILE by the hand and leads him out by the French windows.)*

KAY. Oh, bother Audrey, we can get on quite well...

> *(Their voices die away as they exit.)*

ROYDE. And who is Kay?

TREVES. The present Mrs. Nevile Strange.

> *(MARY enters from the house carrying some sewing. She holds the door open and LADY TRESSILIAN enters using a walking stick. She is a white-haired, aristocratic looking woman of immense gravitas.)*

Good morning, Camilla.

LADY TRESSILIAN. Good morning, Mathew!

> *(She sees ROYDE and greets him with great affection.)*

Well, Thomas, so here you are. I'm very glad to see you.

ROYDE. *(Shyly.)* Very glad to be here.

> *(MARY puts the sewing down and arranges the cushions on the armchair.)*

LADY TRESSILIAN. Tell me all about yourself.

ROYDE. *(Mumbling.)* Nothing to tell.

> *(LADY TRESSILIAN studies his face.)*

LADY TRESSILIAN. You look exactly the same as you did at fourteen. That same boiled owl look. And no more conversation now than you had then.

ROYDE. Never had the gift of the gab.

LADY TRESSILIAN. Then it's time you learnt. Have some sherry? Mathew? Thomas?

ROYDE. Thank you.

(MARY pours two glasses of sherry. **LADY TRESSILIAN** *indicates the sofa.)*

LADY TRESSILIAN. Then go and sit down. Somebody's got to amuse me by bringing me all the gossip.

> *(She sits in the armchair.* **ROYDE** *waits politely then takes a seat on the sofa.)*

Why can't you be more like Adrian? I wish you'd known his brother, Mary, a really brilliant young man, witty, amusing – all the things that Thomas isn't. And don't go grinning at me, Thomas Royde, as though I were praising you. I'm scolding you.

ROYDE. Adrian was certainly the showman of our family.

> *(MARY hands out the sherry.)*

MARY. Did he – was he – killed in the war?

ROYDE. No, he was killed in a motor accident two years ago.

MARY. How dreadful!

TREVES. The impossible way young people drive cars nowadays!

> *(LADY TRESSILIAN picks up her sewing.)*

ROYDE. In his case it was some fault in the steering.

> *(ROYDE takes his pipe from his pocket and looks at* **LADY TRESSILIAN.**)

I'm so sorry, may I?

LADY TRESSILIAN. I wouldn't know you without your pipe. But don't think you can just sit back and puff contentedly while you're here. You've got to exert yourself and help.

ROYDE. *(Surprised.)* Help?

LADY TRESSILIAN. We've got a difficult situation on our hands. Have you been told who's here?

> *(MARY takes a glass of sherry to* **LADY TRESSILIAN.**)

No, no, much too early, pour it back into the decanter.

> *(MARY does so.)*

ROYDE. Yes, I've just heard.

LADY TRESSILIAN. Well, don't you think it's disgraceful?

ROYDE. Well...

TREVES. You'll have to be a little more explicit, Camilla.

LADY TRESSILIAN. I intend to be. When I was a girl such things did not happen. Men had their affairs, naturally, but they did not allow them to break up their married life.

TREVES. Regrettable though the modern point of view may be, one has to accept it, Camilla.

(MARY *takes a seat on the arm of the sofa.*)

LADY TRESSILIAN. That's not the point. We were all delighted when Nevile married Audrey. Such a sweet, gentle girl.

(*She turns to* ROYDE.)

You were all in love with her – you, Adrian and Nevile. Nevile won.

ROYDE. Naturally. He always wins.

(LADY TRESSILIAN *looks at him with frustration.*)

LADY TRESSILIAN. Of all the defeatist...

ROYDE. I don't blame her, Nevile had everything – good looks, first-class athlete, even had a shot at swimming the channel.

TREVES. And all the kudos of that early Everest attempt – never stuck up about it.

ROYDE. *Mens sana in corpore sana.*

LADY TRESSILIAN. Sometimes I think that's the only bit of Latin you men ever learn in your expensive education.

TREVES. My dear Camilla, you must allow for its being invariably quoted by one's housemaster whenever he is slightly embarrassed.

LADY TRESSILIAN. Mary, I wish you wouldn't sit on the arms of chairs, you know how much I dislike it.

MARY. Sorry, Camilla.

(She quickly sits on the sofa.)

LADY TRESSILIAN. Now where was I?

MARY. You were saying that Audrey married Nevile.

LADY TRESSILIAN. Oh, yes. Well, Audrey married Nevile and we were all delighted. Mortimer was particularly pleased, wasn't he, Mathew?

TREVES. Yes, yes.

LADY TRESSILIAN. And they were very happy together until this creature, Kay, came along. How Nevile could leave Audrey for a girl like Kay, I simply cannot imagine.

TREVES. I can – I've seen it happen so often.

LADY TRESSILIAN. Kay is quite the wrong wife for Nevile – no background.

TREVES. But a singularly attractive young woman.

LADY TRESSILIAN. Bad stock. Her mother was notorious all over the Riviera.

ROYDE. What for?

LADY TRESSILIAN. Never you mind. What an upbringing for a girl. Kay made a dead set at Nevile from the moment they met, and never rested until she got him to leave Audrey and go off with her. I blame Kay entirely for the whole thing.

TREVES *(Amused.)* I'm sure you do. You're very fond of Nevile.

LADY TRESSILIAN. Nevile's a fool. Breaking up his marriage for a silly infatuation. It nearly broke poor Audrey's heart.

*(She turns to **ROYDE**.)*

She went to your mother at the vicarage and practically had a nervous breakdown.

ROYDE. Er – yes – I know.

TREVES. When the divorce went through, Nevile married Kay.

LADY TRESSILIAN. If I had been true to my principles I should have refused to receive them here.

TREVES. If one sticks too rigidly to one's principles, one would hardly see anybody.

LADY TRESSILIAN. You're very cynical, Mathew, but it's quite true. I've accepted Kay as Nevile's wife, though I shall never really like her. But I must say, I was dumbfounded and very much upset, wasn't I, Mary?

MARY. Yes, you were, Camilla.

LADY TRESSILIAN. When Nevile wrote asking if he could come home with Kay, under the pretext, if you please, that it would be nice if Audrey and Kay could be friends. *(Scornfully.)* Friends! I said I couldn't entertain such a suggestion for a moment, and that it would be very painful for Audrey.

TREVES. And what did he say to that?

LADY TRESSILIAN. He replied that he had already consulted Audrey and she thought it a good idea.

TREVES. And did Audrey think it a good idea?

LADY TRESSILIAN. Apparently, yes.

> *(She tosses a knot of silk to* **MARY.***)*

Unravel that.

MARY. Well, she said she did. Quite firmly.

LADY TRESSILIAN. But Audrey is obviously embarrassed and unhappy. If you ask me, it's just Nevile being like Henry the Eighth.

ROYDE. Henry the Eighth?

LADY TRESSILIAN. Conscience. Nevile feels guilty about Audrey and is trying to justify himself.

> *(***MARY*** *rises and puts the silk in the work-basket.)*

Oh! I don't understand any of this modern nonsense.

> *(She turns to* **MARY.***)*

Do you?

MARY. In a way.

LADY TRESSILIAN. And you, Thomas?

ROYDE. Understand Audrey – but I don't understand Nevile. It's not like Nevile.

TREVES. I agree. Not like Nevile at all, to go looking for trouble.

MARY. Perhaps it was Audrey's suggestion.

LADY TRESSILIAN. Oh, no. Nevile says it was entirely his idea.

MARY. Perhaps he thinks it was.

      *(***TREVES*** looks curiously at* **MARY.***)*

LADY TRESSILIAN. What a fool the boy is, bringing two women together who are both in love with him.

      *(***ROYDE*** shifts uncomfortably.)*

Audrey has behaved perfectly, but Nevile himself has paid far too much attention to her, and as a result Kay has become jealous, and she has no kind of self-control. It is all most embarrassing.

      (She turns to **TREVES.***)*

Isn't it?

      *(***TREVES*** is gazing towards the French windows and does not hear.)*

Mathew?

TREVES. There is undeniably a certain tension...

LADY TRESSILIAN. I'm glad you admit it.

      (There is a knock on the door leading to the house.)

Who's that?

MARY. Mrs. Barrett, I expect, wanting to know about something.

LADY TRESSILIAN. *(Irritably.)* I wish you could teach these women that they only knock on bedroom doors.

      *(***MARY*** exits into the house.)*

LADY TRESSILIAN. The last so-called butler we had, actually whistled, *"Come into the Garden, Maud"* as he served at the table!

(**MARY** *pops her head round the door.*)

MARY. It's only about the lunch, Camilla. I'll see to it.

(*She exits again.*)

LADY TRESSILIAN. I don't know what I should do without Mary. She's so self-effacing that I sometimes wonder whether she has a self of her own.

TREVES. I know. She's been with you nearly two years now – but what's her background?

LADY TRESSILIAN. Her father was a professor of some kind, I believe. He was an invalid and she nursed him for years. Poor Mary, she's never had any life of her own. And now, perhaps, it's too late.

(*She rises and puts her sewing in the basket.*)

TREVES. I wonder.

(*He looks out the French windows.*)

They're still playing tennis.

(**ROYDE** *rises and looks out as well.*)

LADY TRESSILIAN. Nevile and Kay?

TREVES. No, Kay and that friend of hers from the Easterhead Bay Hotel – young Latimer.

LADY TRESSILIAN. That theatrical looking young man. Just the sort of friend she would have.

TREVES. One wonders what he does for a living.

LADY TRESSILIAN. Lives by his wits, I imagine.

TREVES. Or by his looks. A decorative young man – interesting shaped head. The last man I saw with a head shaped like that was at the Central Criminal Court – a case of brutal assault on an elderly jeweller.

LADY TRESSILIAN. Mathew! Do you mean to tell me?

TREVES. *(Perturbed.)* No, no, no, you misunderstand me. I am making no suggestion of any kind. I was only commenting on a matter of anatomical structure.

LADY TRESSILIAN. Oh, I thought...

TREVES. What reminded me of that was that I met a very old friend of mine this morning, Superintendent Battle of Scotland Yard. He's staying down here on holiday with his nephew who's in the local police.

LADY TRESSILIAN. You and your interest in criminology! The truth is I am thoroughly jumpy. I feel the whole time as though something was going to happen.

TREVES. Yes, there is a suggestion of gunpowder in the air. One little spark might set off an explosion.

LADY TRESSILIAN. Must you talk as though you were Guy Fawkes? Say something cheerful.

TREVES. *(Smiling.)* What can I say? "Men have died from time to time, and worms have eaten them – but not for love."

LADY TRESSILIAN. And he calls that cheerful. I shall go out on the terrace for a little.

> (**TREVES** *looks off out the French windows again.* **LADY TRESSILIAN** *pulls* **ROYDE** *aside.*)

(Confidentially.) Don't make a fool of yourself a second time.

ROYDE. What do you mean?

LADY TRESSILIAN. You know quite well what I mean. Last time, you let Nevile walk off with Audrey under your nose.

ROYDE. Is it likely she'd have preferred me to Nevile?

LADY TRESSILIAN. She might have if you'd asked her!

> (*There is a pause.*)

Are you going to ask her this time?

ROYDE. *(Forcefully.)* You bet your life I am.

LADY TRESSILIAN. Thank God for that.

(**AUDREY** *enters by the French windows. She is very fair but carries a strange air of repressed emotion. With* **ROYDE** *however she is completely natural and happy.*)

AUDREY. Thomas – dear Thomas.

(**ROYDE** *takes* **AUDREY***'s outstretched hands.* **LADY TRESSILIAN** *looks at them warmly for a moment then turns quickly to* **TREVES**.)

LADY TRESSILIAN. Mathew, your arm!

(**TREVES** *offers his arm and they exit by the French windows. There is a pause.*)

AUDREY. It's lovely to see you.

ROYDE. *(Shyly.)* Good to see you.

AUDREY. It's years since you've been home. Don't they give you any leave on rubber plantations?

ROYDE. I was coming home two years ago –

(He breaks off awkwardly.)

AUDREY. Two years ago! And then you didn't.

ROYDE. My dear, you know there were reasons.

AUDREY. *(Affectionately.)* Oh, Thomas, you look just the same as when we last met – pipe and all.

ROYDE. Do I?

AUDREY. Oh, Thomas, I am so glad you've come back. Now, at last, I can talk to someone. Thomas, there's something wrong.

ROYDE. Wrong?

AUDREY. Something's changed about this place. Ever since I arrived, I've felt there was something not quite right. Don't you feel there's something different? No, how can you, you've only just come. The only person who doesn't seem to feel it is Nevile.

ROYDE. Damn Nevile!

AUDREY. You don't like him?

ROYDE. *(Intensely.)* I hate his guts, always have.

(He quickly recovers himself.)

Sorry.

AUDREY. I didn't know...

ROYDE. Lots of things one doesn't know about people.

AUDREY. *(Thoughtfully.)* Yes – lots of things.

ROYDE. Gather there's a spot of bother. What made you come here at the same time as Nevile and his new wife? Did you have to agree?

AUDREY. Yes. Oh, I know you can't understand...

ROYDE. But I do understand. I know all about it.

(**AUDREY** *looks doubtfully at* **ROYDE.**)

(Passionately.) I know exactly what you've been through but it's all past, Audrey – it's over. You must forget the past and think of the future.

(**NEVILE** *enters by the French windows.*)

NEVILE. Hullo, Audrey, where have you been all the morning?

AUDREY. I haven't been anywhere particular.

NEVILE. I couldn't find you anywhere. What about coming down to the beach for a swim before lunch?

AUDREY No, I don't think so.

(She looks among the magazines on the coffee table.)

Have you seen this week's Illustrated London News?

NEVILE. No. Come on, the water will be really warm today.

(**NEVILE** *holds out his hand to her.*)

AUDREY. Actually, I told Mary I'd go into Saltington with her to the shop.

NEVILE. Mary won't mind. Come on, Audrey.

(He takes her hand.)

AUDREY. No, really...

(**KAY** *enters by the French windows.* **NEVILE** *turns to her.*)

NEVILE. I'm trying to persuade Audrey to come bathing.

KAY. Oh? And what does Audrey say?

AUDREY. Audrey says "no".

> *(She withdraws her hand from* **NEVILE***'s and exits into the house.)*

ROYDE. If you'll excuse me, I'll go and unpack.

> *(***ROYDE*** pauses a moment by the bureau bookcase, he selects a book then exits into the house.)*

KAY. So that's that. Coming, Nevile?

NEVILE. Well, I'm not sure.

KAY. *(Impatiently.)* Well, make up your mind.

> *(***NEVILE*** looks off after* **AUDREY***.)*

NEVILE. I'm not sure I won't just have a shower and laze in the garden.

KAY. It's a perfect day for bathing, come on.

NEVILE. What have you done with the boyfriend?

KAY. Ted? I left him on the beach and came up to find you. You can laze on the beach.

> *(She touches his hair. He promptly moves her hand away.)*

NEVILE. With Latimer, I suppose? Doesn't appeal to me a lot.

KAY. You don't like Ted, do you?

NEVILE. Not madly. But if it amuses you to pull him around on a string...

> *(***KAY*** tweaks his ear playfully.)*

KAY. I believe you're jealous.

NEVILE. Of Latimer? Nonsense, Kay.

> *(He pushes her hand away.)*

KAY. Ted's very attractive.

NEVILE. I'm sure he is. He has that lithe South American charm.

KAY. You needn't sneer. He's very popular with women.

NEVILE. Especially with the ones over fifty.

KAY. *(Pleased.)* You are jealous.

NEVILE. My dear, I couldn't care less – he just doesn't count.

KAY. I think you're very rude about my friends. I have to put up with yours.

NEVILE. What do you mean by that?

KAY. Dreary old Lady Tressilian and stuffy old Mr. Treves – and all the rest of them. Do you think I find them amusing?

(Pause.)

Nevile, do we have to stay on here? Can't we go away tomorrow? It's so boring.

NEVILE. We've only just come.

KAY. We've been here four days! Four whole long days. Do let's go, Nevile, please.

NEVILE. Why?

KAY. I want to go. We could easily find some excuse. Please, darling.

NEVILE. Darling, it's out of the question. We came for a fortnight and we're going to stay a fortnight. You don't seem to understand. Sir Mortimer Tressilian was my guardian. I came here for holidays as a boy – Gull's Point was practically my home. Camilla would be terribly hurt.

KAY. *(Impatiently.)* Oh, all right, all right. I suppose we have to suck up to old Camilla because of getting all that money when she dies.

NEVILE. *(Angrily.)* It's not a question of sucking up. I wish you wouldn't look at it like that. She's no control over the money. Old Mortimer left it in trust to come to me and my wife at her death. Don't you realise it's a question of affection?

KAY. Not with me, it isn't, she hates me.

NEVILE. Don't be stupid.

KAY. Yes, she does. She looks down that bony nose of hers at me – and Mary Aldin talks to me as though I were someone she'd just met on a train. They only have me here on sufferance. You don't seem to know what goes on.

NEVILE. They always seem to me to be very nice to you. You imagine things.

KAY. Of course they're polite. But they know how to get under my skin all right. I'm an interloper. That's what they feel.

NEVILE. Well – I suppose that's only natural.

KAY. Oh, yes, I daresay it's quite natural. They're devoted to Audrey, aren't they? Dear, well bred, cool, colourless Audrey. Camilla has never forgiven me for taking Audrey's place. I'll tell you something – Audrey gives me the creeps. You never know what she's thinking.

NEVILE. Oh, nonsense, Kay, don't be absurd.

(He sits heavily on the sofa.)

KAY. Audrey's never forgiven you for marrying me. Once or twice I've seen her looking at you – and the way she looked at you frightened me.

NEVILE. You're prejudiced, Kay. Audrey's been charming. No one could have been nicer.

KAY. It seems like that, but it isn't true. There's something behind it all.

(There is a pause.)

Let's go away, at once, before it's too late.

NEVILE. Don't be melodramatic. I'm not going to upset old Camilla just because you work yourself up into a state about nothing at all.

KAY. It isn't nothing at all! I don't think you know the first thing about your precious Audrey.

*(**LADY TRESSILIAN** and **TREVES** enter by the French windows.)*

NEVILE. *(Furiously.)* She isn't my precious Audrey!

KAY. Isn't she? Anyone would think so, the way you follow her about.

(She catches sight of LADY TRESSILIAN.*)*

LADY TRESSILIAN. Are you going down to bathe, Kay?

KAY. *(Nervously.)* Yes – yes, I was.

LADY TRESSILIAN. Almost high tide. It ought to be very pleasant. What about you, Nevile?

NEVILE. *(Sulkily.)* I don't want to bathe.

*(*LADY TRESSILIAN *turns back to* KAY.*)*

LADY TRESSILIAN. Your friend, I think, is down there waiting for you.

*(*KAY *hesitates a moment, then exits.)*

Nevile, you're behaving very badly. You really must stand up when I come into the room. What's the matter with you – forgetting your manners?

*(*NEVILE *rises quickly.)*

NEVILE. I'm sorry.

LADY TRESSILIAN. You're making us all very uncomfortable. I don't wonder your wife is annoyed.

NEVILE. My wife? Audrey?

LADY TRESSILIAN. Kay is your wife now.

NEVILE. With your high church principles I wonder you admit that fact.

LADY TRESSILIAN. Nevile, you are exceedingly rude.

*(*NEVILE *crosses to* LADY TRESSILIAN, *takes her hand and kisses her on the cheek.)*

NEVILE. I'm very sorry, Camilla. Please forgive me. I'm so worried, I don't know what I'm saying.

LADY TRESSILIAN. *(Affectionately.)* My dear boy, what else could you expect with this stupid idea of being all friends together?

NEVILE. *(Wistfully.)* It still seems to me the sensible way to look at things.

LADY TRESSILIAN. Not with two women like Audrey and Kay.

NEVILE. Audrey doesn't seem to care.

TREVES. How did the matter first come up, Nevile?

NEVILE. *(Eagerly.)* Well, I happened to run across Audrey in London, quite by chance, and she was awfully nice about things – didn't seem to bear any malice or anything like that. While I was talking to her the idea came to me – how sensible it would be if – if she and Kay could be friends – if we could all get together. And it seemed to me that this was the place where it could happen quite naturally.

TREVES. You thought of that all by yourself?

NEVILE. Oh, yes, it was all my idea. And Audrey seemed quite pleased and ready to try.

TREVES. Was Kay equally pleased?

NEVILE. Well, no. I had a spot of bother with Kay. I can't think why – I mean, if anyone were going to object, you'd think it would be Audrey.

LADY TRESSILIAN. Well, I'm an old woman. Nothing people do nowadays seems to make any sense.

> *(She makes for the door leading to the rest of the house. TREVES follows, opening it for her.)*

TREVES. One has to go with the times, Camilla.

LADY TRESSILIAN. I feel very tired. I shall rest before lunch. But you must behave yourself, Nevile – with or without reason, Kay is jealous. I will not have these discordant scenes in my house.

> *(She exits.)*

> *(Offstage.)* Ah, Mary, I shall lie down on the library sofa.

> *(TREVES closes the door and turns to NEVILE.)*

NEVILE. She speaks to me as though I were six!

TREVES. At her age, she doubtless feels you are six.

(**NEVILE** *recovers his temper.*)

NEVILE. Yes, I suppose so. It must be ghastly to be old.

(**TREVES** *pauses slightly.*)

TREVES. It has its compensations, I assure you. (*Dryly.*) There is no longer any question of emotional involvements.

NEVILE. (*Smiling.*) That's certainly something. I suppose I'd better go and make my peace with Kay. I really can't see though why she has to fly off the handle like this. Audrey might very well be jealous of her, but I can't see why she should be jealous of Audrey. Can you?

(**NEVILE** *grins and exits by the French windows.* **TREVES** *looks after him thoughtfully then goes to the waste paper basket. He takes out the pieces of the torn photograph.* **AUDREY** *enters cautiously from the house, looking round for* **NEVILE.**)

AUDREY. What are you doing with my photograph?

TREVES. It seems to have been torn.

AUDREY. Who tore it?

TREVES. Mrs. Barrett, I suppose. That is the name of the woman in the cloth cap who cleans this room? I thought I would put it in here until it can be mended.

(*He puts the pieces of the photograph on the bureau. Their eyes meet for a moment.*)

AUDREY. It wasn't Mrs. Barrett, was it?

TREVES. I have no information, but I should think probably not.

AUDREY. Was it Kay?

TREVES. I told you, I have no information.

(*There is a pause.*)

AUDREY. Oh, dear, this is all very uncomfortable.

TREVES. Why did you come here, my dear?

AUDREY. I suppose – because I always come here at this time.

TREVES. But with Nevile coming here, wouldn't it have been better to have postponed your visit?

AUDREY. I couldn't do that. I have a job, you know. I have to earn my living. I have two weeks holiday and once that is arranged I can't alter it.

TREVES. An interesting job?

AUDREY. Not particularly, but it pays quite well.

TREVES. But, my dear Audrey, Nevile is a very well-to-do man. Under the terms of your divorce he has to make suitable provision for you.

AUDREY. I have never taken a penny from Nevile. I never shall.

TREVES. Quite so. Quite so. Several of my clients have taken that point of view. It has been my duty to dissuade them. In the end, you know, one must be guided by common sense. You have hardly any money of your own, I know. It is only just and right that you should be provided for suitably by Nevile, who can well afford it. Who were your solicitors, because I could –

AUDREY. It's nothing to do with solicitors. I won't take anything from Nevile – anything at all.

TREVES. I see you feel strongly – very strongly.

AUDREY. If you like to put it that way, yes.

TREVES. Was it really Nevile's idea to come here all together?

AUDREY. *(Sharply.)* Of course it was.

TREVES. But you agreed?

AUDREY. I agreed. Why not?

TREVES. It hasn't turned out very well, has it?

AUDREY. That's not my fault.

TREVES. No, it isn't your fault – ostensibly.

AUDREY. What do you mean?

TREVES. I was wondering…

(He breaks off uncomfortably.)

AUDREY. You know, Mr. Treves, sometimes I think I'm just a little frightened of you.

TREVES. Why should you be?

AUDREY. I don't know. You're a very shrewd observer. I sometimes –

(MARY enters from the house.)

MARY. Audrey, will you go to Lady Tressilian? She's in the library.

AUDREY. Yes.

(AUDREY exits into the house. MARY collects the dirty sherry glasses.)

TREVES. Miss Aldin, who do you think is behind this plan of meeting here?

MARY. Audrey.

TREVES. But why?

MARY. I suppose she still cares for him.

TREVES. You think it's that?

MARY. What else can it be? He's not really in love with Kay, you know.

TREVES. These sudden passionate infatuations are very often not of long duration.

MARY. You'd think Audrey would have more pride.

TREVES. In my experience, pride is a word often on women's lips, but they display little sign of it where love affairs are concerned.

MARY. *(Bitterly.)* Perhaps. I wouldn't know.

(She looks off into the garden and sees someone approaching.)

Excuse me.

(She exits into the house. TREVES looks after her thoughtfully. ROYDE enters by the French windows carrying a book.)

TREVES. Ah, Thomas, have you been down to the ferry?

ROYDE. No, I've been reading a detective story.

> *(He holds it up.)*

Not very good. Always seems to me these yarns begin in the wrong place. Begin with the murder. But the murder's not really the beginning.

TREVES. Indeed? Where would you begin?

ROYDE. As I see it, the murder is the end of the story. I mean, the real story begins long before – years before, sometimes. Must do. All the causes and events that bring the people concerned to a certain place, on a certain day, at a certain time. And then, over the top –

> *(He pauses, considering.)*

– zero hour.

TREVES. That is an interesting point of view.

ROYDE. *(Apologetically.)* Not very good at explaining myself, I'm afraid.

TREVES. I think you've put it very clearly, Thomas. All sorts of people converging towards a given spot and hour – all going towards zero.

> *(He pauses briefly.)*

Towards Zero.

Scene Two

(Four days later. Dinner has just finished. A portable record player has been set up with some loose records. The night is very warm, sultry and cloudy. **KAY** *is seated on the sofa, smoking a cigarette. She is in evening dress and looks rather sulky and bored.* **TED LATIMER** *is gazing out the bay window. He is a very dark, good looking man of about twenty-six. His dinner suit fits him a shade too well.)*

KAY. This is what I call a wildly hilarious evening, Ted.

LATIMER. You should have come over to the hotel as I suggested. They've got a dance on. The band's not so hot, but it's fun.

KAY. I wanted to but Nevile wasn't keen.

LATIMER. So you behaved like a dutiful wife.

KAY. Yes, and I've been rewarded by being bored to death.

LATIMER. The fate of most dutiful wives.

(He moves to the record player.)

Aren't there any dance records? We could at least dance.

KAY. There's nothing like that here. Only Mozart and Bach – all classical stuff.

LATIMER. Oh well, at least we've been spared the old battle-axe tonight. Doesn't she ever appear at dinner, or did she just shirk it because I was there?

KAY. Camilla always goes to bed at seven. She's got a groggy heart or something. She has her dinner sent up on a tray.

LATIMER. Not what you'd call a gay life.

(KAY rises abruptly.)

KAY. I hate this place. I wish to God we'd never come here.

LATIMER. Steady, honey. What's the matter?

KAY. I don't know. It's just sometimes I get scared.

LATIMER. That doesn't sound like you, Kay.

KAY. *(Recovering.)* It doesn't, does it? But there's something queer going on. I don't know what, but I'll swear that Audrey's behind it all.

LATIMER. It was a damn silly idea of Nevile's coming here with you at the same time as his ex-wife.

KAY. I don't think it *was* his idea. I'm convinced she put him up to it.

LATIMER. Why?

KAY. I don't know. To cause trouble probably.

LATIMER. What you want is a drink, my girl.

> *(He touches her arm. KAY removes it promptly.)*

KAY. *(Irritably.)* I don't want a drink and I'm not your girl.

LATIMER. You would have been if Nevile hadn't come along.

> *(He pours two glasses of whisky and soda.)*

Where is Nevile, by the way?

KAY. I've no idea.

LATIMER. They're not a very sociable crowd, are they? Audrey's out on the terrace talking to old Treves, and that fellow Royde's strolling about the garden all by himself, puffing at that eternal pipe of his. Nice, cheery lot.

KAY. *(Crossly.)* I wouldn't care a damn if they were all at the bottom of the sea – except Nevile.

LATIMER. I should have felt much happier, darling, if you'd included Nevile.

> *(He picks up the drinks and takes one to KAY.)*

You drink that, my sweet. You'll feel much better.

> *(KAY takes her drink and sips it.)*

KAY. God, it's strong.

LATIMER. More soda?

KAY. No, thanks.

> *(There is a pause.)*

I wish you wouldn't make it so clear you don't like Nevile.

LATIMER. *(Bitterly.)* Why should I like him? He's not my sort. The ideal Englishman – good at sport, modest, good looking, always the little pukka sahib. Getting everything he wants all along the line – even pinched my girl.

KAY. I wasn't your girl.

LATIMER. Yes, you were. If I'd been as well off as Nevile –

KAY. I didn't marry Nevile for his money.

LATIMER. Oh, I know, and I understand – Mediterranean nights and dewy eyed romance...

KAY. I married Nevile because I fell in love with him.

LATIMER. I'm not saying you didn't, my sweet, but his money helped you to fall.

KAY. Do you really think that?

LATIMER. I try to. It helps soothe my injured vanity.

(KAY approaches him affectionately.)

KAY. You're rather a dear, Ted. I don't know what I should do without you, sometimes.

LATIMER. Why try? I'm always around. You should know that by this time. The faithful swain. Or should it be swine? Probably depends which you happen to be – the wife or the husband.

(He kisses KAY's shoulder. MARY enters from the house wearing a plain dinner frock. KAY moves hastily away from LATIMER.)

MARY. *(Pointedly.)* Have either of you seen Mr. Treves? Lady Tressilian wants him.

LATIMER. He's out on the terrace, Miss Aldin.

MARY. Thank you, Mr. Latimer.

(She makes for the French windows.)

Isn't it stifling? I'm sure there's going to be a storm.

LATIMER. I hope it holds off until I get back to the hotel. I didn't bring a coat. I'll get soaked to the skin going over in the ferry if it rains.

MARY. I daresay we could find you an umbrella if necessary, or Nevile could lend you his raincoat.

(She exits by the French windows.)

LATIMER. Interesting woman, that. Bit of a dark horse.

KAY. I feel rather sorry for her. Slaving for that unpleasant old woman and she won't get anything for it, either. All the money comes to me and Nevile.

LATIMER. Perhaps she doesn't know that.

KAY. That would be rather funny.

(They laugh. **AUDREY** *and* **TREVES** *enter by the French windows.* **TREVES** *wears an old-fashioned dinner suit.* **AUDREY,** *an evening dress.* **TREVES** *stops in the doorway and speaks over his shoulder.)*

TREVES. I shall enjoy a little gossip with Lady Tressilian, Miss Aldin. With, perhaps, the remembering of a few old scandals. A touch of malice, you know, adds a certain savour to conversation. Doesn't it, Audrey?

AUDREY. She chooses the person she wants and summons them by a kind of Royal Command.

TREVES. Very aptly put, Audrey. I am always sensible of the royal touch in Lady Tressilian's manner.

(He exits into the house.)

AUDREY. *(Listlessly.)* It's terribly hot, isn't it?

LATIMER. Would you like a drink?

AUDREY. No, thank you. I think I shall go to bed very soon.

(There is a short silence. **NEVILE** *enters from the house. He is wearing a dinner suit and carries a magazine.)*

KAY. What have you been doing all this time, Nevile?

NEVILE. I had a couple of letters to write, thought I might as well get 'em off my chest.

KAY. You might have chosen some other time.

NEVILE. Better the hour, better the deed. By the way, here's the *Illustrated News*. Somebody wanted it.

> (**KAY** *and* **AUDREY** *speak almost at the same moment.*)

KAY. Thank you, Nevile.

AUDREY. Oh! Thank you, Nevile.

> (**NEVILE** *hesitates between them, smiling.*)

KAY. I want it. Give it to me.

> (**AUDREY** *withdraws her hand.*)

AUDREY. Oh, sorry. I thought you were speaking to me, Nevile.

> (**NEVILE** *hesitates for a moment then holds the magazine out to* **AUDREY**.)

NEVILE. *(Quietly.)* Here you are, Audrey.

AUDREY. Oh, but I...

> (**KAY** *tries to suppress her fury. When she speaks her voice is thick with emotion.*)

KAY. It *is* stifling in here.

> (*She rushes to the French windows.*)

Let's go out in the air, Ted. I can't stand being cooped up in this lousy hole any longer.

> (*She almost stumbles as she exits.* **LATIMER** *shoots an angry look at* **NEVILE** *then follows.*)

AUDREY. *(Reproachfully.)* You shouldn't have done that, Nevile.

> (**NEVILE** *tosses the magazine on to the coffee table.*)

NEVILE. Why not?

AUDREY. It was stupid. You'd better go after Kay and apologise.

NEVILE. I don't see why I should apologise.

AUDREY. I think you'd better. You were very rude to your wife.

(**MARY** *enters by the French windows.*)

NEVILE. *(Quietly.)* You're my wife, Audrey. You always will be.

(*He catches sight of* **MARY**.)

Ah, Miss Aldin, are you going up to Lady Tressilian?

MARY. Yes, when Mr. Treves comes down.

(**ROYDE** *enters by the French window.* **NEVILE** *stares at him for a moment then exits after* **KAY**.)

(Wearily.) Oh, dear! I don't think I've ever felt so tired in my life. If Lady Tressilian's bell rings tonight, I'm quite certain I shall never hear it.

(*She sits heavily on the sofa.*)

AUDREY. What bell?

MARY. It rings in my room in case Lady Tressilian should want anything in the night. It's one of those old-fashioned bells on a spring and worked with a wire. It makes a ghastly jangle, but Lady Tressilian insists that it's more reliable than electricity.

(*She yawns.*)

Excuse me, it's this dreadful sultry weather, I think.

AUDREY. You ought to go to bed, Mary. You look worn out.

MARY. I shall as soon as Mr. Treves has finished talking to Lady Tressilian. Then I shall tuck her up for the night and go to bed myself. Oh, dear. It's been a very trying day.

ROYDE. It certainly has.

(**LATIMER** *enters by the French windows.* **AUDREY** *looks at him briefly.*)

AUDREY. Thomas! Let's go on to the terrace.

(She makes for the French windows. **ROYDE** *follows.)*

ROYDE. Yes, I want to tell you about a detective story I've been reading.

(They exit. There is a pause as **LATIMER** *looks after them for a moment.)*

LATIMER. You and I, Miss Aldin, seem to be the odd men out. We must console each other. Can I get you a drink?

MARY. No, thank you.

*(***LATIMER*** *pours himself a drink.)*

LATIMER. One conjugal reconciliation in the rose garden, one faithful swain nerving himself to pop the question. Where do we come in? Nowhere. We're the outsiders.

(He raises his glass.)

Here's to the outsiders. And to hell with all those inside the ringed fence.

MARY. How bitter you are.

LATIMER. So are you.

MARY. Not really.

LATIMER. What's it like, fetching and carrying, running up and down stairs, endlessly waiting on an old woman?

MARY. There are worse things.

LATIMER. I wonder.

(He looks out the French windows after **KAY**. *There is a pause.)*

MARY. You're very unhappy.

LATIMER. Who isn't?

MARY. Have –

(She pauses, considering.)

– you always been in love with Kay?

LATIMER. More or less.

MARY. And she?

LATIMER. I thought so until Nevile came along. Nevile with his money and his sporting record. I could go climbing in the Himalayas if I'd ever had the cash.

MARY. You wouldn't want to.

LATIMER. Perhaps not. *(Sharply.)* What do you want out of life?

> *(**MARY** pauses.)*

MARY. It's almost too late.

LATIMER. But not quite.

MARY. No, not quite. All I want is a little money, not very much, just enough.

LATIMER. Enough for what?

MARY. Enough to have some sort of life of my own before it's too late. I've never had anything.

LATIMER. Do you hate them, too? Those inside the fence?

MARY. *(Violently.)* Hate them – I...

> *(She yawns.)*

No – no, I'm too tired to hate anybody.

> *(**TREVES** enters from the house.)*

TREVES. Ah, Miss Aldin, Lady Tressilian would like you to go to her now if you will be so kind. I think she's feeling sleepy.

MARY. That's a blessing. Thank you, Mr. Treves. I'll go up at once. I shan't come down again so I'll say goodnight now. Good night, Mr. Latimer. Good night, Mr. Treves.

LATIMER. Good night.

> *(**MARY** exits into the house.)*

I must be running along myself. With luck I shall get across the ferry and back to the hotel before the storm breaks.

> *(**ROYDE** enters by the French windows.)*

ROYDE. Are you going, Latimer? Would you like a raincoat?

LATIMER. No, thanks, I'll chance it.

ROYDE. Hell of a storm coming.

TREVES. Is Audrey on the terrace?

ROYDE. *(Curtly.)* I haven't the faintest idea. I'm for bed. Good night.

> (**ROYDE** *exits into the house. A low rumble of thunder is heard.*)

LATIMER. *(Maliciously.)* It would seem that the course of true love has not run smoothly. Was that thunder? Some way away still. I think I'll make it.

TREVES. I'll come with you and bolt the garden gate.

> (*They exit by the French windows.* **AUDREY** *is heard off calling to them.*)

AUDREY. *(Offstage.)* Good night.

> (*She enters rather quickly and makes for the door leading to the rest of house. Another rumble of thunder is heard.* **NEVILE** *quickly follows her on.*)

NEVILE. Audrey.

AUDREY. I'm going to bed, Nevile. Good night.

NEVILE. Don't go yet. I want to talk to you.

AUDREY. *(Nervously.)* I think you'd better not.

NEVILE. I must. I've got to. Please listen to me, Audrey.

AUDREY. I'd rather you didn't.

NEVILE. That means you know what I'm going to say.

> (*She does not reply.*)

Audrey, can't we go back to where we were? Forget everything that has happened?

> (*There is a slight pause.*)

AUDREY. Including Kay?

NEVILE. Kay will be sensible.

AUDREY. What do you mean by sensible?

NEVILE. I shall tell her the truth – that you are the only woman I've ever loved. That is the truth, Audrey. You've got to believe that.

AUDREY. *(Desperately.)* You loved Kay when you married her.

NEVILE. My marriage to Kay was the biggest mistake I ever made. I realise now what a damned fool I've been. I –

(**KAY** *enters by the French windows.*)

KAY. Sorry to interrupt this touching scene, but I think it's about time I did.

NEVILE. Kay, listen...

KAY. *(Furiously.)* Listen! I've heard all I want to hear – too much.

AUDREY. I'm going to bed. Good night.

(*She makes to exit into the house.* **KAY** *follows her.*)

KAY. That's right. Go to bed! You've done all the mischief you wanted to do, haven't you? But you're not going to get out of it as easily as all that. I'll deal with you after I've had it out with Nevile.

AUDREY. *(Coldly.)* It's no concern of mine. Good night.

(*She exits into the house. There is a flash of lightning and a peal of thunder.* **KAY** *looks after* **AUDREY**.)

KAY. Of all the damned, cool –

NEVILE. Look here, Kay – Audrey had absolutely nothing to do with this. It's not her fault. Blame me if you like.

KAY. *(Angrily.)* And I do like. What sort of a man do you think you are?

(*Her voice rises.*)

You leave your wife, come bald-headed after me – get your wife to divorce you. Crazy about me one minute, tired of me the next. Now I suppose you want to go back to that whey-faced, mewling, double-crossing little cat!

NEVILE. (*Angrily.*) Stop that, Kay.

KAY. That's what she is. A crafty, cunning, scheming, little –

(**NEVILE** *grabs her by the shoulders.*)

NEVILE. Stop it!

KAY. Leave me alone!

(*She releases herself.*)

What the hell do you want?

NEVILE. I can't go on. I'm every kind of worm you like to call me. But it's no good, Kay. I can't go on. I think, really, I must have loved Audrey all the time. I've only just realised it. My love for you was – was a kind of madness. But it's no good – you and I don't belong. It's better to cut our losses.

KAY. (*Quietly.*) What exactly are you suggesting, Nevile?

NEVILE. We can get a divorce. You can divorce me for desertion.

KAY. You'd have to wait three years for it.

NEVILE. I'll wait.

KAY. And then, I suppose, you'll ask dear, sweet, darling Audrey to marry you all over again? Is that the idea?

NEVILE. If she'll have me.

KAY. She'll have you all right. And where do I come in?

NEVILE. Naturally, I'll see you're well provided for.

(**KAY** *starts to lose control.*)

KAY. Cut out the bribes! Listen to me, Nevile. I'll not divorce you!

(*She beats her hands savagely on his chest.*)

You fell in love with me and you married me, and I'm not going to let you go back to that sly little bitch who's got her hooks into you again!

(**NEVILE**'s *temper starts to fray.*)

NEVILE. Shut up, Kay, for God's sake! You can't make this kind of scene here.

KAY. *(Hysterically.)* She meant this to happen. It's what she's been playing for. She's probably gloating over her success now! But she's not going to bring it off. You'll see what I can do!

> (**TREVES** *enters by the French windows, taking in the scene.* **KAY** *sobs hysterically and storms out, slamming the door behind her. There is a brilliant flash of lightning and a rolling peal of thunder as the storm bursts.)*

ACT II

Scene One

*(Early the following morning. Sun streams in through the open French windows. The butler's tray has been removed. **ROYDE** enters. He is sucking at his pipe which appears to have become blocked. He takes a penknife from his pocket and gently probes the bowl. **TREVES** enters from the house.)*

TREVES. Good morning, Thomas.

ROYDE. Morning. Going to be another lovely day by the look of it.

TREVES. Yes. I thought possibly the storm might have broken up the spell of fine weather, but it has only removed that oppressive heat which is all to the good. You've been up for hours as usual, I presume?

ROYDE. Since just after six. Been for a walk along the cliffs. Only just got back, as a matter of fact.

TREVES. Nobody else appears to be about yet. Not even Miss Aldin.

ROYDE. Um.

TREVES. Possibly she is fully occupied attending to Lady Tressilian. I should imagine she may be rather upset after that unfortunate incident last night.

*(**ROYDE** blows down his pipe.)*

ROYDE. Bit of a rumpus, wasn't there?

TREVES. You have a positive genius for understatement, Thomas. That unpleasant scene between Nevile and Kay –

43

ROYDE. *(Surprised.)* Nevile and Kay? The row I heard was between Nevile and Lady Tressilian.

TREVES. When was this?

ROYDE. Must have been about twenty past ten. They were going at it hammer and tongs. Couldn't help hearing. My room's practically opposite hers, you know.

TREVES. *(Troubled.)* Dear, dear, this is news to me.

ROYDE. Thought that was what you meant.

TREVES. No, no, I was referring to a most distressing scene that took place in here earlier, to part of which I was a reluctant witness. That unfortunate young woman – er – Kay, had a fit of violent hysterics.

ROYDE. What was the row about?

TREVES. I'm afraid it was Nevile's fault.

ROYDE. That doesn't surprise me. He's been behaving like a damn fool.

TREVES. I entirely agree. His conduct has been most reprehensible.

ROYDE. Was Audrey mixed up in the row?

TREVES. She was the cause of it.

> (**KAY** *enters quickly from the house with her handbag. She looks subdued and tired.*)

KAY. Oh. Good – good morning.

TREVES. Good morning, Kay.

ROYDE. Good morning.

KAY. *(Nervously.)* We're – we're the only ones up, aren't we?

TREVES. I think so. I haven't seen anyone else. I breakfasted in – er – solitary state.

ROYDE. Haven't had mine yet. Think I'll go and hunt some up. Have you had breakfast?

KAY. No. I've only just come down. I – I don't want any breakfast. I feel like hell.

ROYDE. Um – could eat a house, myself.

> (*He makes to exit.*)

See you later.

(*He exits into the house.* **KAY** *turns to* **TREVES** *tentatively.*)

KAY. Mr. Treves. I – I'm afraid I behaved rather badly last night.

TREVES. It was very natural that you should be upset.

KAY. I lost my temper and I said a lot of – of foolish things.

TREVES. We are all apt to do that at times. You had every provocation. Nevile was, in my opinion, very much to blame.

KAY. He was led into it. Audrey's been determined to cause trouble between Nevile and me ever since we came here.

TREVES. I don't think you're being quite fair to her.

KAY. She planned this, I tell you. She knows that Nevile's always – always felt guilty at the way he treated her.

TREVES. No, no, I'm sure you're wrong.

KAY. No, no, I'm not wrong. You see, Mr. Treves, I went over it all in the night. Audrey thought that if she could get us all here together and – and pretend to be friendly and forgiving that she could get him back. She's worked on his conscience. Pale and aloof, creeping about like a – like a grey ghost. She knew what effect that would have on Nevile. He's always reproached himself because he thought he'd treated her badly.

(*There is a pause.* **KAY** *sits on the sofa hopelessly.*)

Right from the beginning – or nearly the beginning – Audrey's shadow has been between us. Nevile couldn't quite forget about her, she was always there at the back of his mind.

TREVES. You can hardly blame her for that.

KAY. Oh, don't you see? She knew how Nevile felt. She knew what the result would be if they were thrown together again.

TREVES. I think you are giving her credit for more cunning than she possesses.

KAY. You're all on her side – all of you!

TREVES. My dear Kay!

KAY. You'd like to see Nevile go back to Audrey. I'm the interloper, I don't belong. Nevile said so last night and he was right. Camilla's always disliked me, she's put up with me for Nevile's sake. I'm supposed to see everyone's point of view but my own. What I feel or think doesn't matter. If my life is all smashed up it's just too bad, but it doesn't matter. It's only Audrey who matters.

TREVES. No, no, no.

(**KAY**'s voice rises.)

KAY. Well, she's not going to smash up my life! I don't care what I do to stop it, but I will. I'll make it impossible for Nevile to go back to her.

(**NEVILE** enters from the house.)

NEVILE. What's the matter now? More trouble?

KAY. What do you expect after the way you behaved last night?

NEVILE. It was you who made all the fuss, Kay. I was prepared to talk the matter over calmly –

KAY. (Rising.) Calmly! Did you imagine that I was going to accept your suggestion that I should divorce you, and leave the way clear for Audrey, as if – as if you were inviting me to – to go to a dance?

NEVILE. No, but at least you needn't behave in this hysterical fashion when you're staying in other people's houses. For goodness sake control yourself and try to behave properly.

KAY. Like she does, I suppose?

NEVILE. At any rate, Audrey doesn't make an exhibition of herself.

KAY. She's turning you against me – just as she intended.

NEVILE. Look here, Kay, this isn't Audrey's fault. I told you that last night. I explained the situation. I was quite open and honest about it.

KAY. Open and honest!

NEVILE. Yes. I can't help feeling the way I do.

KAY. How do you suppose I feel? You don't care about that, do you?

TREVES. *(Interposing.)* I really think, Nevile, that you should very seriously consider your attitude in this – er – matter. Kay is your wife. She has certain rights of which you cannot deprive her in this – this cavalier manner.

NEVILE. I admit that, but I'm willing to do the – the right thing.

KAY. The right thing!

TREVES. Furthermore it is hardly the – er – proper procedure to discuss this under Lady Tressilian's roof. It is bound to upset her very seriously. My sympathies are entirely with Kay, but I think you both have a duty to your hostess and to your fellow guests. I suggest that you postpone any further discussion of the matter until your visit here has terminated.

NEVILE. *(Shamed.)* I suppose you're right, Mr. Treves – yes, of course, you're right. I'm willing. What do you say, Kay?

KAY. As long as Audrey doesn't try and –

NEVILE. *(Sharply.)* Audrey hasn't tried anything!

TREVES. Ssh!

> *(He turns to* **KAY**.*)*

I think, my dear, you would be well advised to agree to my suggestion. It is only a question of a few more days.

KAY. *(Ungraciously.)* Oh, very well then.

NEVILE. *(Relieved.)* Well, that's that. I'm going to get some breakfast.

> *(He glances out of the bay window.)*

NEVILE. We might all go sailing later on. There's quite a good breeze.

(*He looks at* **TREVES.***)*

Would you like to come?

TREVES. I'm afraid I'm a little too old for that sort of thing.

NEVILE. What about you, Kay?

KAY. What about Ted? We promised him we'd go over this morning.

NEVILE. There's no reason why he shouldn't come, too. I'll get hold of Royde and Audrey and see what they think of the idea. It should be lovely out in the bay.

(**AUDREY** *enters from the house looking worried.*)

AUDREY. (*Anxiously.*) Mr. Treves, what do you think we ought to do? We can't wake Mary.

NEVILE. Can't wake her? What do you mean?

AUDREY. Just that. When Mrs. Barrett came, she took up Mary's morning tea as usual. Mary was fast asleep. Mrs. Barrett drew the curtains and called to her, but Mary didn't wake up, so she left the tea on the bedside table. She didn't bother much, but when Mary didn't come down to fetch Camilla's tea, Mrs. Barrett went up again. Mary's tea was stone cold and she was still asleep.

TREVES. She was very tired last night, Audrey.

AUDREY. But this isn't a natural sleep, Mr. Treves. It can't be. Mrs. Barrett shook her hard and she didn't wake. I went in to Mary and I tried to wake her, too. There's definitely something wrong with her.

NEVILE. Do you mean she's unconscious?

AUDREY. I don't know. She looks very pale and she just lies there like a log.

KAY. Perhaps she took some sleeping pills.

AUDREY. That's what I thought, but it's so unlike Mary.

(*She turns to* **TREVES.***)*

What shall we do?

TREVES. I think you should get a doctor. She may be ill.

NEVILE. I'll go and phone Lazenby and get him to come at once.

(*He exits quickly into the house.*)

TREVES. Have you told Lady Tressilian, Audrey?

AUDREY. No, not yet. I didn't want to disturb her. They're making her some fresh tea in the kitchen. I'm going to take it up. I'll tell her then.

TREVES. I sincerely hope it's nothing serious.

KAY. She's probably taken an overdose of sleeping stuff.

TREVES. That could be extremely serious.

AUDREY. I can't imagine Mary doing such a thing.

(**ROYDE** *enters from the house.*)

ROYDE. I heard Strange telephoning Dr. Lazenby. What's the matter?

AUDREY. It's Mary. She's still asleep and we can't get her to wake up. Kay thinks she may have taken an overdose of some drug.

KAY. Something like that must have happened or you'd be able to wake her.

ROYDE. Sleeping stuff, do you mean? Shouldn't think she'd have needed anything like that last night. She was dog tired.

TREVES. I'm sure she wouldn't take any sort of drug, you know – in case the bell rang.

KAY. Bell?

ROYDE. There's a bell in her room. Lady Tressilian always rings it if she wants anything in the night.

(*He turns to* **AUDREY.**)

Remember she was telling us about it last night.

AUDREY. Mary wouldn't take anything that would stop her hearing the bell, in case it was urgent.

(**NEVILE** *enters quickly.*)

NEVILE. Lazenby's coming round right away.

AUDREY. Oh, good. Before he gets here I'd better go and see about Camilla's tea. She'll be wondering what's happened.

NEVILE. Can I help?

AUDREY. No, thank you. I can manage.

        (**AUDREY** *exits into the house.*)

ROYDE. I wonder if it could be some kind of heart attack.

NEVILE. It's not much use conjecturing, is it? Lazenby'll be able to tell us. Poor old Mary. I don't know what will happen if she's really ill.

TREVES. It would be disastrous. Lady Tressilian relies on Mary for everything.

KAY. (*Hopefully.*) I suppose we shall all have to pack up and go?

        (**NEVILE** *turns to* **KAY**.)

NEVILE. Perhaps it isn't anything very serious after all.

ROYDE. Must be something pretty bad if she can't be wakened.

TREVES. It can't take Dr. Lazenby very long to get here and then we shall know. He lives a very short distance away.

NEVILE. He ought to be here in about ten minutes, I should think.

TREVES. Possibly he will be able to relieve all our minds. I trust so.

NEVILE. No good looking on the black side of things, anyway.

KAY. Always the perfect optimist, aren't you, Nevile?

NEVILE. Well, things usually work out all right.

ROYDE. They certainly do for you.

        (*There is a pause.*)

NEVILE. I don't quite know what you mean by that, Thomas.

ROYDE. I should have thought it was obvious.

NEVILE. What are you insinuating?

ROYDE. *(Angrily.)* I'm not insinuating anything. I'm stating facts.

TREVES. Ssh!

> (**TREVES** *stands between the two men and tries to change the subject.*)

Do you think – er – we ought to see if there is anything we could do to – er – help. Lady Tressilian might wish –

NEVILE. If Camilla wants us to do anything she'll soon say so. I wouldn't interfere unless she does, if I were you.

> (*A blood curdling scream is heard, off.* **ROYDE** *exits hurriedly into the house. There is a short pause then* **AUDREY**, *completely dazed, is carried into the room by* **ROYDE**.)

AUDREY. Camilla – Camilla...

TREVES. My dear! What's the matter?

> (**AUDREY** *speaks almost in a whisper.*)

AUDREY. It's – Camilla.

NEVILE. *(Surprised.)* Camilla? What's wrong with her?

AUDREY. She's – she's dead.

KAY. Oh, no, no.

NEVILE. It must have been her heart.

AUDREY. No – it – it wasn't her heart.

> (*She presses a shaking hand to her eyes then bursts out hysterically.*)

There's blood all over her head! She's been murdered!

> (*She sobs hopelessly.*)

Don't you understand? She's been murdered.

Scene Two

(Two hours later. The furniture has been moved to make the room more suitable for police interrogations. A card table has been set up with some chairs. On the table is a small tray with a jug of water, glasses and a box of cigarettes. **TREVES** *is seen looking around the room briefly before* **SUPERINTENDENT BATTLE** *enters from the house. He is a big man, aged about fifty.)*

TREVES. Ah. Battle.

BATTLE. That's fixed up, sir.

TREVES. It was all right, was it, Battle?

BATTLE. Yes, sir. The Chief Constable got through to the Yard. As I happened to be on the spot they've agreed to let me handle the case.

TREVES. I'm very glad. It's going to make it easier having you instead of a stranger. Pity to have spoilt your holiday though.

BATTLE. Oh, I don't mind that, sir. I'll be able to give my nephew a hand. It'll be his first murder case, you see.

TREVES. Yes – yes, I've no doubt he will find your experience of great help.

BATTLE. It's a nasty business.

TREVES. Shocking, shocking.

BATTLE. I've seen the doctor. Two blows were struck. The first was sufficient to cause death. The murderer must have struck again to make sure – or in a blind rage.

TREVES. Horrible. I can't believe it could have been anyone in the house.

BATTLE. Afraid it was, sir. We've been into all that. No entry was forced. All the doors and windows were fastened this morning as usual. And then there's the drugging of Miss Aldin, that must have been an inside job.

TREVES. How is she?

BATTLE. Still sleeping it off. She was given a pretty heavy dose. It looks like careful planning on somebody's part. Lady Tressilian might have pulled that bell which rings in Miss Aldin's room, if she'd been alarmed. That had to be taken care of, so Miss Aldin was doped.

TREVES. *(Troubled.)* It still seems to me quite incredible.

BATTLE. We'll get to the bottom of it, sir, in the end. Death occurred, according to the doctor, between ten-thirty and midnight. Not earlier than ten-thirty, not later than midnight. That should be a help.

TREVES. Yes, yes. And the weapon used was a niblick?

BATTLE. Yes, sir. Thrown down by the bed, blood-stained and with white hairs sticking to it.

> (**TREVES** *turns away in repulsion.*)

I shouldn't have deduced a niblick from the appearance of the wound, but apparently the sharp edge of the club didn't touch the head. The doctor says it was the rounded part of the club that hit her.

TREVES. The – er – murderer was incredibly stupid, don't you think, to leave the weapon behind?

BATTLE. Probably lost his head. It happens.

TREVES. Possibly – yes, possibly. I suppose there are no fingerprints?

BATTLE. Sergeant Pengelly is attending to that now, sir. I doubt if it's going to be as easy as that.

> (**INSPECTOR LEACH** *enters from the house. He is a man of about forty. He speaks with a slight Cornish accent and carries a niblick golf club.*)

LEACH. See here, Uncle. Pengelly has brought up a beautiful set of dabs on this – clear as day.

BATTLE. *(Warningly.)* Be careful how you go handling that, my boy.

LEACH. It's all right, we've got photographs. Got specimens of the blood and hair, too.

(He shows the club to **BATTLE.***)*

LEACH. What do you think of these dabs? Clear as clear, aren't they?

*(***BATTLE*** inspects the fingerprints.)*

BATTLE. They're clear enough. What a fool!

(He shows the club to **TREVES.***)*

LEACH. That's so, to be sure.

BATTLE. All we've got to do now, my lad, is ask everyone nicely and politely if we may take their fingerprints – no compulsion, of course. Everyone will say "yes" and one of two things will happen. Either none of the prints will agree, or else...

LEACH. It'll be in the bag, eh?

*(***BATTLE*** nods.)*

TREVES. Doesn't it strike you as extremely odd, Battle, that the – er – murderer should have been so foolish as to leave such a damning piece of evidence behind – actually on the scene of the crime?

BATTLE. I've known 'em do things equally foolish, sir.

(He hands the club back to **LEACH.***)*

Well, let's get on with it. Where's everybody?

LEACH. In the library, Pollock is going through all their rooms. Except Miss Aldin's, of course, she's still sleeping off the effects of that dope.

BATTLE. We'll have 'em in here one at a time.

(He turns to **TREVES.***)*

Which Mrs. Strange was it who discovered the murder?

TREVES. Mrs. Audrey Strange.

BATTLE. Oh, yes. Difficult when there are two Mrs. Stranges. Mrs. Audrey Strange is the divorced wife, isn't she?

TREVES. Yes. I explained to you the – er – situation.

BATTLE. Yes, sir. Funny idea of Mr. Strange's. I should have thought that most men –

(**KAY** *enters quickly from the house. Upset and slightly hysterical, she makes for the French windows.* **BATTLE** *blocks her path.*)

KAY. I'm not going to stay cooped up in that damned library any longer. I want some air and I'm going out. You can do what the hell you like about it.

BATTLE. Just a minute, Mrs. Strange. There's no reason why you shouldn't go out if you wish, but it'll have to be later.

KAY. I want to go now.

BATTLE. I'm afraid that's impossible.

KAY. You've no right to keep me here. I haven't done anything.

BATTLE. *(Soothingly.)* No, no, of course you haven't. But you see, there'll be one or two questions we'll have to ask you.

KAY. What sort of questions? I can't help you. I don't know anything about it.

(**BATTLE** *turns to* **LEACH**.)

BATTLE. Get Benson, will you, Jim?

(**LEACH** *nods and exits into the house.*)

Now, you just sit down here, Mrs. Strange and relax.

(*He indicates a chair at the card table.* **KAY** *sits reluctantly.*)

KAY. I've told you I don't know anything. Why do I have to answer a lot of questions when I don't know anything?

BATTLE. *(Apologetically.)* We've got to interview everybody, you see, it's just part of the routine. Not very pleasant for you, or for us, but there you are.

KAY. *(Impatiently.)* Oh, well, all right.

(**P.C BENSON** *enters, followed by* **LEACH**. **BENSON** *is a young man, fair and very quiet.*

He nods to **BATTLE** *and takes out a notebook and pencil.)*

BATTLE. Now, just tell us about last night, Mrs. Strange.

KAY. What about last night?

BATTLE. What did you do – say from after dinner, onwards?

KAY. I had a headache. I – I went to bed quite early.

BATTLE. How early?

KAY. I don't know exactly. It was about a quarter to ten, I think.

*(**TREVES** interposes gently.)*

TREVES. Ten minutes to ten.

KAY. Was it? I wouldn't know to the minute.

BATTLE. We'll take it was ten minutes to ten.

*(He signs to **BENSON**, who makes a note.)*

Did your husband accompany you?

KAY. No.

BATTLE. What time did he come to bed?

KAY. I've no idea. You'd better ask him that.

LEACH. The door between your room and your husband's is locked. Was it locked when you went to bed?

KAY. Yes.

LEACH. Who locked it?

KAY. I did.

BATTLE. Was it usual for you to lock it?

KAY. No.

BATTLE. Why did you do so last night, Mrs. Strange?

*(**KAY** does not reply. There is a pause. **TREVES** gives a little cough.)*

TREVES. I should tell them, Kay.

KAY. I suppose if I don't, you will. Oh, well, then, you can have it. Nevile and I had a row – a flaming row.

*(**LEACH** looks to **BENSON**, who makes a note.)*

I was furious with him. I went up to bed and locked the door because I was still in a flaming rage with him.

BATTLE. I see. What was the trouble about?

KAY. Does it matter? I don't see how it concerns –

BATTLE. You're not compelled to answer, if you'd rather not.

KAY. Oh, I don't mind. My husband has been behaving like a perfect fool. It's all that woman's fault, though.

BATTLE. What woman?

KAY. Audrey. His first wife. It was she who got him to come here in the first place.

BATTLE. I understood that it was Mr. Strange's idea.

KAY. Well, it wasn't. It was hers.

BATTLE. But why should Mrs. Audrey Strange have suggested it?

KAY. To cause trouble, I suppose. Nevile thinks it was his own idea – poor innocent. But he never thought of such a thing until he met Audrey in the park one day in London, and she put the idea into his head and made him believe he'd thought of it himself. I've seen her scheming mind behind it from the first. She's never taken *me* in.

BATTLE. Why should she be so anxious for you all to come here together?

KAY. *(Angrily.)* Because she wanted to get hold of Nevile again, that's why. She's never forgiven him for going off with me. This is her revenge. She got him to fix it so that we'd be here together and then she got to work on him. She's been doing it ever since we arrived. She's clever, damned clever. She knows just how to look pathetic and elusive. Poor sweet, injured little kitten with all her blasted claws out.

TREVES. Kay – Kay.

BATTLE. I see. Surely, if you felt so strongly, you could have objected to this arrangement of coming here?

KAY. Do you think I didn't try? Nevile was set on it. He insisted.

BATTLE. But you're quite sure it wasn't his idea?

KAY. I'm positive. That white-faced little cat planned it all.

TREVES. You have no actual evidence on which to base such an assertion, Kay.

KAY. *(Rising.)* I know, I tell you, and you know it, too, though you won't admit it! Audrey's been –

BATTLE. Come and sit down, Mrs. Strange.

(**KAY** *does so, reluctantly.*)

Did Lady Tressilian approve of the arrangement?

KAY. She didn't approve of anything in connection with me. Audrey was her pet. She disliked me for taking Audrey's place with Nevile.

BATTLE. Did you quarrel with Lady Tressilian?

KAY. No.

BATTLE. After you'd gone to bed, Mrs. Strange, did you hear anything? Any unusual sounds in the house?

KAY. I didn't hear anything. I was so upset I took some sleeping stuff. I fell asleep almost at once.

BATTLE. What kind of sleeping stuff?

KAY. They're little blue capsules. I don't know what's in them.

(**BATTLE** *looks to* **BENSON.** *A note is made.*)

BATTLE. You didn't see your husband after you went up to bed?

KAY. No, no, no. I've already told you that I locked the door.

(**BATTLE** *takes the niblick from* **LEACH** *and shows it to* **KAY.**)

BATTLE. Have you ever seen this before, Mrs. Strange?

(**KAY** *shrinks away, revolted.*)

KAY. How – how horrible. Is that what – what it was done with?

BATTLE. We believe so. Have you any idea to whom it belongs?

(**KAY** *shakes her head.*)

KAY. There are packets of golf clubs in the house. Mr. Royde's, Nevile's, mine –

BATTLE. This is a man's club. It wouldn't be one of yours.

KAY. Then it must be...

(*She pauses.*)

I don't know.

BATTLE. I see.

(*He places the niblick neatly against the card table.*)

Thank you, Mrs. Strange, that's all for the present.

(**KAY** *rises and makes for the French windows.*)

LEACH. There's just one other thing.

(**KAY** *turns.*)

Would you object to letting Detective Sergeant Pengelly take your fingerprints?

KAY. My fingerprints?

BATTLE. It's just a matter of routine, Mrs. Strange. We're asking everybody.

KAY. I don't mind anything so long as I don't have to go back to that menagerie in the library.

LEACH. I'll arrange for Sergeant Pengelly to take your fingerprints in the breakfast room.

(**KAY** *looks closely at* **TREVES** *for a moment, then exits reluctantly into the house.* **LEACH** *follows her off.* **BENSON** *closes his notebook and waits stolidly.*)

BATTLE. Benson. Go and ask Pollock if he saw some small blue capsules in Mrs. Strange's room – Mrs. Kay Strange. I want a specimen of them.

BENSON. Yes, sir.

BATTLE. Come back here when you've done that.

BENSON. Yes, sir.

>   *(He exits into the house.)*

TREVES. Do you think the same drug was used to – er – dope Miss Aldin?

BATTLE. It's worth checking up on. Would you mind telling me, sir, who stands to gain by Lady Tressilian's death?

TREVES. Lady Tressilian had very little money of her own. The late Sir Mortimer Tressilian's estate was left in trust for her during her lifetime. On her death it is to be equally divided between Nevile and his wife.

BATTLE. Which wife?

TREVES. His first wife.

BATTLE. Audrey Strange?

TREVES. Yes. The bequest is quite clearly worded, "Nevile Henry Strange, and his wife, Audrey Elizabeth Strange, née Standish." The subsequent divorce makes no difference whatever to the bequest.

BATTLE. Mrs. Audrey Strange is, of course, fully aware of that?

TREVES. Certainly.

BATTLE. And the present Mrs. Strange, does she know that she gets nothing?

TREVES. Really, I cannot say. *(Doubtfully.)* Presumably her husband has made it clear to her.

BATTLE. If he hadn't she might be under the impression that she was the one who benefited.

TREVES. It's possible, yes.

BATTLE. Is the amount involved a large one, sir?

TREVES. Quite considerable. Approaching one hundred thousand pounds.

BATTLE. Whew! That's quite something, even in these days.

>   **(LEACH** *enters carrying a crumpled dinner jacket.)*

LEACH. I say, take a look at this. Pollock has just found it bundled down in the bottom of Nevile Strange's wardrobe.

(He points to the sleeve.)

Look at these stains. That's blood, or I'm Marilyn Monroe.

(BATTLE takes the jacket.)

BATTLE. You're certainly not Marilyn Monroe, Jim. It's spattered all up the sleeve as well. Any other suits in the room?

LEACH. Dark grey pinstripe hanging over a chair. And there's a lot of water round the wash basin on the floor – quite a pool of it. Looks as if it had slopped over.

BATTLE. Such as might have been made if he'd washed the blood off his hands in the devil of a hurry, eh?

LEACH. Yes.

(He takes some tweezers from his pocket and picks a hair on the inside of the collar.)

BATTLE. Hairs! A woman's fair hair on the inside of the collar.

LEACH. Some on the sleeve, too.

BATTLE. Red ones, these. Mr. Strange seems to have had his arm round one wife and the other one's head on his shoulder.

LEACH. Quite a Mormon. Looks bad for him, don't it?

BATTLE. We'll have to have the blood on this tested later to see if it's the same group as Lady Tressilian's.

LEACH. I'll try and arrange it, Uncle.

TREVES. *(Perturbed.)* I can't believe – I really can't believe that Nevile, whom I've known all his life, is capable of such a terrible act. There must be a mistake.

BATTLE. I hope so, I'm sure, sir.

(He turns to LEACH.)

We'll have Mr. Royde in next.

(**LEACH** *nods and exits.* **BATTLE** *hangs the jacket on one of the chairs.*)

TREVES. I'm quite sure there must be some innocent explanation, Battle, for that stained dinner jacket. Quite apart from lack of motive, Nevile is –

BATTLE. Fifty thousand pounds is a pretty good motive, sir, to my mind.

TREVES. But Nevile is well off. He's not in need of money.

BATTLE. There may be something we know nothing about, sir.

(**BENSON** *enters from the house. He carries a small round box.*)

BENSON. Pollock found the pills, sir, here you are.

(*He hands the box to* **BATTLE.**)

BATTLE. These are the things. I'll get the doctor to tell us whether they contain the same stuff that was given to Miss Aldin.

(**ROYDE** *enters from the house.*)

ROYDE. You want to see me?

BATTLE. Yes, Mr. Royde. Will you sit down, sir?

ROYDE. Rather stand.

BATTLE. Just as you like.

(**BENSON** *takes out his notebook and pencil.*)

I'd like you to answer one or two questions, if you've no objection.

ROYDE. No objection at all. Nothing to hide.

BATTLE. I understand that you have only just returned from Malaya, Mr. Royde?

ROYDE. That's right. First time I've been home for seven years.

BATTLE. You've known Lady Tressilian for a long time?

ROYDE. Ever since I was a boy.

BATTLE. Can you suggest a reason why anyone should want to kill her?

ROYDE. No.

BATTLE. How long have you known Mr. Nevile Strange?

ROYDE. Practically all my life.

BATTLE. Do you know him sufficiently well to be aware if he was worried over money?

ROYDE. No, but I shouldn't think so. Always seems to have plenty.

BATTLE. If there was any trouble like that he wouldn't be likely to confide in you?

ROYDE. Very unlikely.

BATTLE. What time did you go to bed last night, Mr. Royde?

ROYDE. Round about half past nine, I should think.

BATTLE. That seems to be very early.

ROYDE. Always go to bed early. Like to get up early.

BATTLE. I see. Your room is practically opposite Lady Tressilian's, isn't it?

ROYDE. Practically.

BATTLE. Did you go to sleep immediately when you went to bed?

ROYDE. No. Finished a detective story I was reading. Not very good – it seems to me they always –

BATTLE. Yes, yes. Were you still awake at half past ten?

ROYDE. Yes.

BATTLE. Did you – this is very important, Mr. Royde – did you hear any unusual sounds round about that time?

(**ROYDE** *does not reply.*)

I'll repeat that question. Did you –

ROYDE. There's no need. I heard you.

BATTLE. Well, Mr. Royde?

ROYDE. Heard a noise in the attic over my head, rats, I expect. Anyway, that was later.

BATTLE. I don't mean that.

(**ROYDE** *looks at* **TREVES.**)

ROYDE. (*Reluctantly.*) There was a bit of a rumpus.

BATTLE. What sort of rumpus?

ROYDE. Well, an argument.

BATTLE. An argument? Who was the argument between?

ROYDE. Lady Tressilian and Strange.

BATTLE. Lady Tressilian and Mr. Strange were quarrelling?

ROYDE. Well, yes. I suppose you'd call it that.

BATTLE. It's not what I would call it, Mr. Royde. Do *you* call it that?

ROYDE. Yes.

BATTLE. Thank you. What was this quarrel about?

ROYDE. Didn't listen. Not my business.

BATTLE. But you are quite sure they were quarrelling?

ROYDE. Sounded like it. Their voices were raised pretty high.

BATTLE. Can you place the time exactly?

ROYDE. About twenty past ten I should think.

BATTLE. Twenty past ten. You didn't hear anything else?

ROYDE. Strange slammed the door when he left.

BATTLE. You heard nothing more after that?

ROYDE. Only rats.

> (*He busies himself with his pipe.*)

BATTLE. Never mind the rats.

> (*He picks up the niblick.*)

Does this belong to you, Mr. Royde?

> (**ROYDE** *is engrossed with his pipe and does not reply.*)

Mr. Royde!

> (**ROYDE** *looks at the niblick.*)

ROYDE. No. All my clubs have got T.R. scratched on the shaft.

BATTLE. Do you know to whom it does belong?

ROYDE. No idea.

(BATTLE replaces the niblick.)

BATTLE. We shall want to take your fingerprints, Mr. Royde. Have you any objection to that?

ROYDE. Not much use objecting, is it? Your man's already done it.

(BENSON laughs quietly.)

BATTLE. Thank you, then, Mr. Royde. That's all for the present.

ROYDE. Do you mind if I go out for a bit? Feel like some fresh air. Only out on the terrace, if you want me.

BATTLE. That'll be quite all right, sir.

ROYDE. Thanks.

(ROYDE exits by the French windows.)

BATTLE. The evidence seems to be piling up against Mr. Strange, sir.

TREVES. It's incredible – incredible.

(LEACH enters from the house.)

LEACH. *(Jubilantly.)* The fingerprints are Nevile Strange's all right.

BATTLE. That would seem to clinch it, Jim. He leaves his weapon, he leaves his fingerprints – I wonder he didn't leave his visiting card.

LEACH. Been easy, hasn't it?

TREVES. It can't have been Nevile. There must be a mistake.

BATTLE. It all adds up. We'll see what Mr. Strange has to say, anyhow. Bring him in, Jim.

(LEACH exits into the house.)

TREVES. I don't understand it. I'm sure there's something wrong. Nevile's not a complete and utter fool. Even if he were capable of committing such a brutal act, which I refuse to believe, would he have left all this damning evidence strewn about so carelessly?

BATTLE. Well, sir, apparently he did. You can't get away from facts.

(**NEVILE** *and* **LEACH** *enter from the house.*
NEVILE *looks worried and nervous. He stands
a moment in the doorway.* **BATTLE** *indicates a
chair at the card table.*)

BATTLE. Come and sit down, Mr. Strange.

NEVILE. Thank you.

(*He sits.*)

BATTLE. We should like you to answer certain questions,
but it's my duty to caution you that you are not bound
to answer these questions unless you wish.

NEVILE. Go ahead. Ask me anything you wish.

BATTLE. You realise that anything you say will be taken
down in writing and may subsequently be used in
evidence in a court of law?

NEVILE. Are you threatening me?

BATTLE. No, no, Mr. Strange – warning you.

TREVES. Superintendent Battle is obliged to conform to the
regulations, Nevile. You need say nothing unless you
wish to.

NEVILE. Why shouldn't I wish to?

TREVES. (*Significantly.*) It might be wiser not to.

NEVILE. Nonsense! Go ahead, Superintendent. Ask me
anything you like.

(**TREVES** *shakes his head despairingly.*
BENSON *takes out his notebook.*)

BATTLE. Are you prepared to make a statement?

NEVILE. If that's what you call it. I'm afraid, though, I can't
help you very much.

BATTLE. Will you begin by telling us exactly what you did
last night? From dinner onwards?

NEVILE. Let me see. Immediately after dinner I went up
to my room and wrote a couple of letters – I'd been
putting them off for a long time and I thought I might
as well get them done. When I finished I came down
here.

BATTLE. What time would that be?

NEVILE. I suppose it was about a quarter past nine. That's as near as dammit, anyhow.

(**BATTLE** *helps himself to a cigarette.*)

BATTLE. I'm so sorry.

(*He offers one to* **NEVILE.**)

NEVILE. No, thank you.

BATTLE. What did you do after that?

NEVILE. I talked to – to Kay, my wife, and Ted Latimer.

BATTLE. Latimer? Who's he?

NEVILE. A friend of ours who's staying at the Easterhead Bay Hotel. He'd come over for dinner. He left soon after and everybody else went off to bed.

BATTLE. Including your wife?

NEVILE. Yes, she was feeling a bit off colour.

BATTLE. I understand there was some sort of unpleasantness?

(**NEVILE** *looks to* **TREVES.**)

NEVILE. Oh, you've heard about that, have you? It was purely a domestic quarrel. Can't have anything to do with this horrible business.

BATTLE. I see. After everybody else had gone to bed, what did you do then?

NEVILE. I was a bit bored. It was still fairly early and I decided to go across to the Easterhead Bay Hotel.

BATTLE. In the storm? It had broken by this time, surely?

NEVILE. Yes, it had. But it didn't worry me. I went upstairs to change –

BATTLE. (*Interrupting.*) Change into what, Mr. Strange?

NEVILE. I was wearing a dinner jacket. As I proposed to take the ferry across the river and it was raining pretty heavily, I changed.

(*He pauses.*)

Into a grey pinstripe, if it interests you.

BATTLE. Go on, Mr. Strange.

> (**NEVILE** *shows signs of increasing nervousness.*)

NEVILE. I went up to change, as I said. I was passing Lady Tressilian's door, which was ajar, when she called, "Is that you, Nevile?" and asked me to come in. I went in and – and we chatted for a bit.

BATTLE. How long were you with her?

NEVILE. About twenty minutes, I suppose. When I left her I went to my room, changed, and hurried off. I took the latchkey with me because I expected to be late.

BATTLE. What time was it then?

NEVILE. About half past ten, I should think. I just caught the ten thirty-five ferry and went across to the Easterhead side of the river. I had a drink or two with Latimer at the hotel and watched the dancing. Then we had a game of billiards. In the end I found I'd missed the last ferry back. It goes at one-thirty. Latimer very decently got out his car and drove me home. It's fifteen miles round by road, you know.

> (*He pauses.*)

We left the hotel at two o'clock and reached here at half past. Latimer wouldn't come in for a drink, so I let myself in and went straight up to bed.

> (**BATTLE** *and* **TREVES** *exchange a glance.*)

BATTLE. During your conversation with Lady Tressilian was she quite normal in her manner?

NEVILE. Oh, yes, quite.

BATTLE. What did you talk about?

NEVILE. This and that.

BATTLE. Amiably?

NEVILE. Of course.

BATTLE. (*Smoothly.*) You didn't have a violent quarrel?

> (**NEVILE** *rises, angrily.*)

NEVILE. What the devil do you mean?

BATTLE. You'd better tell the truth, Mr. Strange. I'll warn you – you were overheard.

NEVILE. Well, we did have a difference of opinion. She – she disapproved of my behaviour over – over Kay and – and my first wife. I may have got a bit heated, but we parted on perfectly friendly terms. *(Angrily.)* I didn't bash her over the head because I lost my temper if that's what you think.

> (**BATTLE** *picks up the niblick.*)

BATTLE. Is this your property, Mr. Strange?

> (**NEVILE** *looks it over.*)

NEVILE. Yes. It's one of Walter Hudson's niblicks from St. Egbert's.

BATTLE. This is the weapon we think was used to kill Lady Tressilian. Have you any explanation for your fingerprints being on the grip?

NEVILE. But of course they would be, it's my club. I've often handled it.

BATTLE. Any explanation, I mean, for the fact that your fingerprints show that you were the last person to have handled it?

NEVILE. That's not true. It can't be. Somebody could have handled it after me – someone wearing gloves.

BATTLE. Nobody could have handled it in the sense you mean – by raising it to strike – without blurring your own marks.

> (**NEVILE** *stares at the niblick in sudden realisation.*)

NEVILE. It can't be! Oh, God!

> *(There is a pause.)*

It isn't that? It simply isn't true. You think I killed her, but I didn't. I swear I didn't. There's some horrible mistake.

(BATTLE replaces the niblick.)

TREVES. Can't you think of any explanation to account for those fingerprints, Nevile?

(BATTLE picks up the dinner jacket.)

NEVILE. No. No – I can't think of anything.

BATTLE. Can you explain why the cuffs and sleeve of this dinner jacket, your dinner jacket, are stained with blood?

(NEVILE speaks in a horror-stricken whisper.)

NEVILE. Blood? It couldn't be.

TREVES. You didn't, for instance, cut yourself?

(NEVILE rises, pushing his chair back violently.)

NEVILE. No – no, of course I didn't! It's fantastic, simply fantastic! It's none of it true.

BATTLE. The facts are true enough, Mr. Strange.

NEVILE. But why should I do such a dreadful thing? It's unthinkable – unbelievable. I've known Lady Tressilian all my life. Mr. Treves, you don't believe it, do you? You don't believe that I would do a thing like this?

(BATTLE replaces the jacket.)

TREVES. No, Nevile, I can't believe it.

NEVILE. I didn't. I swear I didn't. What reason could I have?

BATTLE. I believe that you inherit a great deal of money on Lady Tressilian's death, Mr. Strange.

NEVILE. You mean, you think that...? It's ridiculous! I don't need money. I'm quite well off. You've only to enquire at my bank.

BATTLE. We shall check up on that. But there may be some reason why you suddenly require a large sum of money – some reason unknown to anyone except yourself.

NEVILE. There's nothing of the sort.

BATTLE. As to that, we shall see.

NEVILE. Are you going to arrest me?

BATTLE. Not yet, we propose to give you the benefit of the doubt.

NEVILE. *(Bitterly.)* You mean that you've made up your mind I did it, but you want to be sure of my motive so as to clinch the case against me. That's it, isn't it? My God! It's like some awful dream.

> *(He looks to* **TREVES**.*)*

Like being caught in a trap and you can't get out.

> *(He pauses, distraught.)*

Do you want me any more now? I'd like to – to get out by myself and think over all this. It's been rather a shock.

BATTLE. We've finished with you for the present, sir.

NEVILE. Thank you.

> *(He makes for the French windows.)*

BATTLE. Don't go too far away, though, will you, sir?

NEVILE. You needn't worry. I shan't try and run away if that's what you mean.

> *(He glances off.)*

I see you've taken your precautions, anyway.

> *(He exits.)*

LEACH. He did it all right.

BATTLE. I don't know, Jim. If you want the truth, I don't like it. I don't like any of it. There's too much evidence against him. Besides, it doesn't quite fit. Lady Tressilian calls him into the room, and he goes happening to have a niblick in his hand. Why?

LEACH. So as to bash her over the head.

BATTLE. Meaning it's premeditated? All right, he's drugged Miss Aldin – but he can't count on her being asleep so soon. He couldn't count on anybody being asleep so soon.

LEACH. Well then, say he's cleaning his clubs. Lady T calls him. They have a row, he loses his temper and bashes her with the club he just happens to be holding.

BATTLE. That doesn't account for the drugging of Mary Aldin. And she was drugged, the doctor says so. Of course, she could have drugged herself.

LEACH. Why?

(**BATTLE** *turns to* **TREVES**.)

BATTLE. Is there any possible motive in Miss Aldin's case?

TREVES. Lady Tressilian left her a legacy – not a very large one – a few hundreds a year. As I told you, Lady Tressilian had very little personal fortune.

BATTLE. A few hundreds a year.

TREVES. I agree. An inadequate motive.

BATTLE. *(Sighing.)* Well, let's see the first wife. Jim, get Mrs. Audrey Strange.

(**LEACH** *exits.*)

There's something peculiar about this business, sir. A mixture of cold premeditation and unpremeditated violence, and the two don't mix.

TREVES. Exactly, Battle. The drugging of Miss Aldin suggests premeditation –

BATTLE. And the way the murder was carried out looks as though it was done in a fit of blind rage. Yes, sir. It's all wrong.

TREVES. Did you notice what he said about a trap?

BATTLE. *(Thoughtfully.)* "A trap."

(**LEACH** *enters from the house and holds the door open.* **AUDREY** *follows. She is very pale but completely composed.* **LEACH** *exits back into the house, closing the door behind him.*)

AUDREY. You wish to see me?

BATTLE. Yes. Please sit down, Mrs. Strange.

(**AUDREY** *sits.*)

You've already told me how you came to make the discovery, so we needn't go into that again.

AUDREY. Thank you.

BATTLE. I'm afraid, however, that I shall have to ask you several questions that you may find embarrassing. You are not compelled to answer them unless you like.

AUDREY. I don't mind. I only wish to help.

BATTLE. First of all, then, will you tell us what you did after dinner last night?

AUDREY. I was on the terrace for some time talking to Mr. Treves. Then Miss Aldin came out to say that Lady Tressilian would like to see him in her room, and I came in here. I talked to Kay and Mr. Latimer and, later, to Mr. Royde and Nevile. Then I went up to bed.

BATTLE. What time did you go to bed?

AUDREY. I think it was about half past nine. I'm not sure of the time exactly. It may have been a little later.

BATTLE. There was some sort of trouble between Mr. Strange and his wife, I believe. Were you mixed up in that?

AUDREY. Nevile behaved very stupidly. I think he was rather excited and overwrought. I left them together and went to bed. I don't know what happened after that, naturally.

BATTLE. Did you go to sleep at once?

AUDREY. No. I was reading for some little while.

BATTLE. And you heard nothing unusual during the night?

AUDREY. No, nothing. My room is on the floor above Cam – Lady Tressilian's. I wouldn't have heard anything.

(**BATTLE** *shows* **AUDREY** *the niblick.*)

BATTLE. I'm sorry, Mrs. Strange, we believe this was used to kill Lady Tressillan. It has been identified by Mr. Strange as his property. It also bears his fingerprints.

(**AUDREY** *draws in a sharp breath.*)

AUDREY. Oh, you – you're not suggesting that it was Nevile?

BATTLE. Would it surprise you?

AUDREY. Very much. I'm sure you're quite wrong, if you think so. Nevile would never do a thing like that. Besides, he had no reason.

BATTLE. Not if he wanted money very urgently?

AUDREY. He wouldn't. He's not an extravagant person, he never has been. You're quite, quite wrong if you think it was Nevile.

BATTLE. You don't think he would be capable of violence in a fit of temper?

AUDREY. Nevile? Oh, no!

BATTLE. I don't want to pry into your private affairs, Mrs. Strange, but will you explain why you are here?

AUDREY. *(Surprised.)* Why? I always come here at this time.

BATTLE. But not at the same time as your ex-husband.

AUDREY. He did ask me if I'd mind.

BATTLE. It was his suggestion?

AUDREY. Oh, yes.

BATTLE. Not yours?

AUDREY. No.

BATTLE. But you agreed?

AUDREY. Yes, I agreed. I didn't feel that I could very well refuse.

BATTLE. Why not? You must have realised that it might be embarrassing?

AUDREY. Yes, I did realise that.

BATTLE. You were the injured party?

AUDREY. I beg your pardon?

BATTLE. It was you who divorced your husband?

AUDREY. Oh, I see – yes.

BATTLE. Do you feel any animosity towards him, Mrs. Strange?

AUDREY. No, none at all.

BATTLE. You have a very forgiving nature.

(**AUDREY** *does not reply.*)

Are you on friendly terms with the present Mrs. Strange?

AUDREY. I don't think she likes me very much.

BATTLE. Do you like her?

AUDREY. I really don't know her.

BATTLE. You are quite sure it was not your idea – this meeting?

AUDREY. Quite sure.

BATTLE. I think that's all, Mrs. Strange, thank you.

AUDREY. Thank you.

(*She rises then hesitates.*)

(*Nervously.*) I would just like to say – you think Nevile did this – that he killed her because of the money? I'm quite sure that isn't so. Nevile never cared much about money. I do know that. I was married to him for several years, you see. It – it isn't Nevile. I know my saying this isn't of any value as evidence, but I do wish you would believe it.

(*She turns quickly and exits into the house.*)

BATTLE. It's difficult to know what to make of her, sir. I've never seen anyone so devoid of emotion.

TREVES. H'm. She didn't show any, Battle, but it's there – some very strong emotion. I thought...but I may have been wrong –

(**MARY,** *assisted by* **LEACH,** *enters. She wears a dressing gown and sways drowsily as she walks.*)

Mary!

BATTLE. Miss Aldin! You shouldn't –

(**TREVES** *leads her to a chair at the card table.*)

LEACH. She insisted on seeing you, Uncle.

MARY. *(Faintly.)* I'm all right. I just feel a little dizzy still. I had to come. They told me something about your suspecting Nevile. Is that true? Do you suspect Nevile?

BATTLE. Who told you so?

MARY. The cook. She brought me up some tea. She heard them talking in this room. And then I came down and I saw Audrey and she said it was so.

(She looks from one to the other.)

BATTLE. *(Evasively.)* We are not contemplating an arrest at this moment.

MARY. But it can't have been Nevile. I had to come and tell you. Whoever did it, it wasn't Nevile. That I know.

BATTLE. How do you know?

MARY. Because I saw her – Lady Tressilian – alive after Nevile had left the house.

BATTLE. What?

MARY. My bell rang, you see. I was terribly sleepy. I could only just get up. It was a minute or two before half past ten. As I came out of my room Nevile was in the hall below. I looked over the banisters and saw him. He went out of the front door and slammed it behind him. Then I went in to Lady Tressilian.

BATTLE. And she was alive and well?

MARY. Yes, of course. She seemed a little upset and said Nevile had shouted at her.

(BATTLE turns to LEACH.)

BATTLE. Get Mr. Strange.

(LEACH exits by the French windows.)

What did Lady Tressilian say exactly?

MARY. She said –

(She thinks.)

Oh, dear, what did she say? She said, "Did I ring for you? I can't remember doing so. Nevile has behaved very badly, losing his temper, shouting at me. I feel most upset." I gave her some aspirin and some hot milk from the thermos and she settled down. Then I went back to bed. I was desperately sleepy. Dr. Lazenby asked me if I'd taken any sleeping pills –

BATTLE. Yes, we know –

> (**NEVILE** *and* **LEACH** *enter by the French windows.* **KAY** *follows.*)

You are a very lucky man, Mr. Strange.

NEVILE. Lucky? Why?

BATTLE. Miss Aldin saw Lady Tressilian alive after you left the house, and we've already established you were on the ten thirty-five ferry.

NEVILE. *(Bewildered.)* Then that lets me out? But the blood stained jacket – the niblick with my fingerprints on it?

BATTLE. Planted. Very ingeniously planted. Blood and hair smeared on the niblick head. Someone put on your jacket to commit the crime and then stuffed it away in your wardrobe to incriminate you.

NEVILE. But why? I can't believe it.

BATTLE. *(Impressively.)* Who hates you, Mr. Strange? Hates you so much that they wanted you to be hanged for a murder you didn't commit?

> *(There is a pause.)*

NEVILE. *(Shaken.)* Nobody – nobody.

> (**ROYDE** *enters by the French windows.* **NEVILE** *turns to look at him.*)

ACT III

Scene One

*(The next morning, about eleven o'clock. Most of the furniture has been replaced in its original position. The sun is shining brightly and all the windows are open. **ROYDE** gazes out onto the bay. **MARY** enters by the French windows. She looks worried and preoccupied.)*

MARY. Oh, dear!

ROYDE. Anything the matter?

*(**MARY** laughs with a slight note of hysteria.)*

MARY. Nobody but you could say a thing like that, Thomas. A murder in the house and you just say "Is anything the matter?"

ROYDE. I meant anything fresh.

MARY. Oh, I know what you meant. It's really a wonderful relief to find anyone so gloriously just-the-same-as-usual as you are.

ROYDE. Not much good, is it, getting all het up over things?

MARY. No, you're very sensible, of course. It's how you manage to do it, beats me.

ROYDE. I'm not so close to things as you are.

MARY. That's true. I don't know what we should have done without you. You've been a tower of strength.

ROYDE. The human buffer, eh?

MARY. The house is still full of policemen.

ROYDE. Yes, I know. Found one in the bathroom this morning. Had to turf him out before I could shave.

MARY. I know – you come across them in the most unexpected places. They're looking for something.

(She shivers.)

It was a very near thing for poor Nevile, wasn't it?

ROYDE. Yes, very near. *(Grimly.)* I can't help feeling pleased he's had a bit of a kick in the pants. He's always so damned complacent.

MARY. It's just his manner.

ROYDE. He's had the devil's own luck. If it had been some other poor chap with all that evidence piled up against him, he wouldn't have had a hope.

MARY. It must have been someone from outside.

ROYDE. It wasn't. They've proved that. Everything was fastened up and bolted in the morning.

*(**MARY** examines the catch of the bay window.)*

Besides, what about your dope? That must have been someone in the house.

MARY. I just can't believe it could have been one of us.

*(**LATIMER** enters by the French windows.)*

LATIMER. Hullo, Royde. Good morning, Miss Aldin. I'm looking for Kay. Do you know where she is?

MARY. I think she's up in her room, Mr. Latimer.

LATIMER. I thought she might like to come and have lunch at the hotel. Not very cheerful for her here, under the circumstances.

MARY. You can hardly expect us to be very cheerful after what's happened, can you?

LATIMER. That's what I meant. It's different for Kay, though, you know. The old girl didn't mean so much to her.

MARY. Naturally. She hasn't known Lady Tressilian as long as we have.

LATIMER. Nasty business. I've had the police over at the hotel this morning.

MARY. What did they want?

LATIMER. Checking up on Strange, I suppose. They asked me all sorts of questions. I told them he was with me from after eleven until half past two, and they seemed satisfied. Lucky thing for him that he decided to follow me over to the hotel that night, wasn't it?

ROYDE. *(Rising.)* Very lucky. I'm going upstairs, Latimer. I'll tell Kay you're here, if I can find her.

LATIMER. Thanks.

> (**ROYDE** *exits into the house.* **LATIMER** *looks after him for a moment.*)

A queer chap. Always seems to be keeping himself bottled up and afraid the cork might come out. Is Audrey going to reward, at long last, the dog-like devotion of a lifetime?

MARY. *(Annoyed.)* I don't know, and it's no business of ours.

> (*She hesitates.*)

When you saw the police did they say anything? I mean did you get any idea as to who they suspect now?

LATIMER. They weren't making any confidences.

MARY. I didn't suppose they were, but I thought, perhaps, from the questions they asked –

> (**KAY** *enters from the house.*)

KAY. Hullo, Ted. It was sweet of you to come over.

LATIMER. I thought you could probably do with a bit of cheering up, Kay.

KAY. My God, how right you were. It was bad enough before in this house, but now...

LATIMER. What about a run in the car and lunch at the hotel – or anywhere else you like?

KAY. I don't know what Nevile's doing...

LATIMER. I'm not asking Nevile, I'm asking you.

KAY. I couldn't come without Nevile, Ted. I'm sure it would do him good to get away from here for a bit.

LATIMER. All right, bring him along if you want to, Kay. I'm easy.

KAY. Where is Nevile, Mary?

MARY. I don't know. I think he's in the garden somewhere.

KAY. I'll see if I can find him. I won't be long, Ted.

(KAY *exits by the French windows.*)

LATIMER. (*Angrily.*) What she sees in him I can't think. He's treated her like dirt.

MARY. I think she'll forgive him.

LATIMER. She shouldn't. Now she's got her share of the old girl's money, she can go where she pleases, do what she likes. She's got a chance now of having a life of her own.

MARY. Can one ever really have a life of one's own? Isn't that just the illusion that lures us on, thinking, planning for a future that will never really exist?

LATIMER. That wasn't what you were saying the other night.

MARY. I know. But that seems a long time ago. So much has happened since then.

LATIMER. Specifically, one murder.

MARY. You wouldn't talk so flippantly about murder if –

LATIMER. If what, Miss Aldin?

MARY. If you had been as close to murder as I have.

LATIMER. This time it is better to be an outsider.

(KAY *and* NEVILE *enter by the French windows.* KAY *looks a little annoyed.*)

KAY. It's no good, Ted. Nevile won't come, so we can't go.

NEVILE. I don't see very well how we can. It's awfully nice of you, Latimer, but it would hardly be the thing, would it, after what's happened?

LATIMER. I don't see what harm it would do to go out to lunch – you've got to eat.

NEVILE. We can eat here.

(KAY *huffs, exasperated.*)

Hang it all, Kay, we can't go joy riding about the country. The inquest hasn't been held yet.

LATIMER. If you feel like that about it, Strange, I suppose we'd better call it off.

MARY. Perhaps you would care to stay and lunch with us, Mr. Latimer?

LATIMER. Well, that's very nice of you, Miss Aldin.

NEVILE. Yes, do, Latimer.

KAY. Will you, Ted?

LATIMER. Thanks, I'd like to.

MARY. You'll have to take pot luck. I'm afraid the domestic arrangements are just a little disorganised with the police popping in and out of the kitchen every two minutes.

LATIMER. If it's going to be any trouble?

MARY. Oh, no, it'll be no trouble at all.

*(**AUDREY** enters from the house.)*

AUDREY. Has anyone seen Mr. Treves this morning?

NEVILE. I haven't seen him since breakfast.

MARY. He was talking to the Inspector in the garden about half an hour ago. Do you want him particularly?

AUDREY. Oh, no, I just wondered where he was.

*(**NEVILE** looks off through the French windows.)*

NEVILE. They're coming now. Not Mr. Treves, Superintendent Battle and Inspector Leach.

MARY. *(Nervously.)* What do you think they want now?

*(They all wait nervously. **BATTLE** and **LEACH** enter. **LEACH** carries a long brown paper parcel.)*

BATTLE. Hope we're not disturbing you all. There are one or two things we'd like to know about.

NEVILE. I should have thought you'd exhausted everything by now, Superintendent.

BATTLE. Not quite, Mr. Strange.

(He takes a small, chamois-leather glove from his pocket.)

BATTLE. There's this glove, for instance. Who does it belong to?

(They all stare at the glove without answering. BATTLE turns to AUDREY.)

Is it yours, Mrs. Strange?

AUDREY. No, no, it isn't mine.

BATTLE. Miss Aldin?

MARY. I don't think so. I have none of that colour.

(BATTLE turns to KAY.)

BATTLE. What about you?

KAY. No. I'm sure it doesn't belong to me.

BATTLE. Perhaps you'd just slip it on? It's the left hand glove.

(KAY tries on the glove but it is too small.)

Will you try, Miss Aldin?

(MARY does so, but again it is too small. BATTLE turns finally to AUDREY.)

I think you'll find it fits you all right. Your hand is smaller than the other two ladies'.

(AUDREY reluctantly takes the glove.)

NEVILE. *(Sharply.)* She's already told you that it isn't her glove.

BATTLE. Perhaps she made a mistake or forgot.

AUDREY. It may be mine, gloves are so alike, aren't they?

BATTLE. Try it on, Mrs. Strange.

(AUDREY slips the glove on. It fits perfectly.)

It seem as if it is yours at any rate. It was found outside your window, pushed down into the ivy with the other one that goes with it.

AUDREY. I – I don't know – anything about it.

(She hastily removes the glove and gives it to **BATTLE.***)*

NEVILE. Look here, Superintendent, what are you driving at?

BATTLE. Perhaps I might have a word with you privately, Mr. Strange?

(**LATIMER** *moves to the French windows.*)

LATIMER. Come on, Kay, let's go out in the garden.

(They exit.)

BATTLE. There's no need to disturb everybody.

(He turns to **NEVILE.***)*

Isn't there somewhere else we could...?

MARY. I was just going, in any case. You coming with me, Audrey?

AUDREY. Yes – yes.

(She nods in a dazed, frightened manner. **MARY** *puts her arm around her and they exit into the house.)*

NEVILE. Now, Superintendent? What's this absurd story about gloves outside Audrey's window?

BATTLE. It's not absurd, sir. We've found some very curious things in this house.

NEVILE. Curious? What do you mean by curious?

BATTLE. Give us the exhibit, Jim.

(**LEACH** *extracts a heavy, steel-headed poker from his parcel and hands it to* **BATTLE.***)*

Old-fashioned Victorian fire iron.

NEVILE. You think that this –

BATTLE. – was what was really used? Yes, Mr. Strange, I do.

NEVILE. But why? There's no sign...

BATTLE. Oh, it's been cleaned, and put back in the grate of the room where it belonged. But you can't remove bloodstains as easily as all that. We found traces all right.

NEVILE. *(Hoarsely.)* Whose room was it in?

BATTLE. We'll come to that presently. I've got another question to ask you. That dinner jacket you wore last night, it's got fair hairs on the inside of the collar and on the shoulders. Do you know how they got there?

NEVILE. No.

BATTLE. They're a lady's hairs, sir. Fair hairs. There are several red hairs, as well, on the sleeves.

NEVILE. Those would be my wife's – Kay's. You are suggesting that the others are Audrey's?

BATTLE. Oh, they are, sir. Unquestionably, We've had them compared with hairs from her brush.

NEVILE. Very likely they are. What about it? I remember I caught my cuff button in her hair the other night on the terrace.

LEACH. In that case the hairs would be on the cuff, sir. Not on the inside of the collar.

NEVILE. What are you insinuating?

BATTLE. There are traces of powder, too, inside the jacket collar. Primavera Naturelle – a very pleasant scented powder and expensive. It's no good telling me that you use it, Mr. Strange, because I shan't believe you. And Mrs. Kay Strange uses Orchid Sun Kiss. Mrs. Audrey Strange uses Primavera Naturelle.

NEVILE. Supposing she does?

BATTLE. It seems obvious that on some occasion Mrs. Audrey Strange actually wore your dinner jacket. It's the only reasonable way the hairs and the powder could have got inside the collar. You've seen the glove that was found in the ivy outside her window. It's hers all right. It was the left hand glove. Here's the right hand one.

(He takes the glove from his pocket and holds it up. It is crumpled and stained with dried blood.)

NEVILE. *(Huskily.)* What – what's that on it?

BATTLE. Blood, Mr. Strange.

*(He holds the glove out to **LEACH**, who takes it.)*

Blood of the same group as Lady Tressilian's. An unusual blood group.

NEVILE. Good God! Are you suggesting that Audrey – Audrey would make all these elaborate preparations to kill an old lady she had known for years? So that she could get hold of that money?

(His voice rises.)

Audrey?

*(**ROYDE** enters quickly from the house.)*

ROYDE. Sorry to interrupt, but I'd like to be in on this.

NEVILE. *(Annoyed.)* Do you mind, Thomas? This is all rather private.

ROYDE. I'm afraid I don't care about that. You see, I heard Audrey's name mentioned –

NEVILE. *(Angrily.)* What the hell has Audrey's name got to do with you?

ROYDE. What has it to do with you, if it comes to that? I came here meaning to ask her to marry me, and I think she knows it. What's more, I mean to marry her.

NEVILE. I think you've got a damn nerve!

ROYDE. You can think what you like. I'm stopping here.

*(**BATTLE** coughs.)*

NEVILE. Oh, all right! Sorry, Superintendent, for the interruption.

*(He turns back to **ROYDE**, reluctantly.)*

NEVILE. The Superintendent is suggesting that Audrey – Audrey committed a brutal assault on Camilla and killed her. Motive – money.

BATTLE. I didn't say the motive was money. I don't think it was, though fifty thousand pounds is a very sizeable motive. No, I think that this crime was directed against you, Mr. Strange.

NEVILE. *(Startled.)* Me?

BATTLE. I asked you yesterday who hated you. The answer, I think, is Audrey Strange.

NEVILE. Impossible. Why should she? I don't understand.

BATTLE. Ever since you left her for another woman, Audrey Strange has been brooding over her hatred of you. In my opinion – and strictly off the record – I think she's become mentally unbalanced. I daresay we'll have these high-class doctors saying so with a lot of long words. Killing you wasn't enough to satisfy her hate. She decided to get you hanged for murder.

NEVILE. *(Shaken.)* I'll never believe that.

BATTLE. She wore your dinner jacket, she planted your niblick, smearing it with Lady Tressilian's blood and hair. The only thing that saved you was something she couldn't foresee. Lady Tressilian rang her bell for Miss Aldin after you'd left.

NEVILE. It isn't true – it can't be true! You've got the whole thing wrong. Audrey's never borne a grudge against me. She's always been gentle – forgiving.

BATTLE. It's not my business to argue with you, Mr. Strange. I asked for a word in private because I wanted to prepare you for what's about to happen. I'm afraid I shall have to caution Mrs. Audrey Strange and ask her to accompany me.

NEVILE. You mean you're going to arrest her?

BATTLE. Yes, sir.

NEVILE. You can't – you can't – it's preposterous!

ROYDE. Pull yourself together, Strange. Don't you see that the only thing that can help Audrey now is for you to forget all your ideas of chivalry and come out with the truth?

NEVILE. The truth? You mean...?

ROYDE. I mean the truth about Audrey and Adrian. I'm sorry, Superintendent, but you've got your facts wrong. Strange didn't leave Audrey for another woman. She left him. She ran away with my brother Adrian. Then Adrian was killed in a car accident on his way to meet her. Strange behaved very decently to Audrey. He arranged for her to divorce him and agreed to take the blame.

NEVILE. *(Hopelessly.)* I didn't want her name dragged through the mud. I didn't know anyone knew.

ROYDE. Adrian wrote to me and told me all about it just before he was killed.

(He turns to **BATTLE.***)*

You see, that knocks your motive out, doesn't it? Audrey has no cause to hate Strange. On the contrary, she has every reason to be grateful to him.

NEVILE. *(Eagerly.)* Royde's right, He's right. That cuts out the motive. Audrey can't have done it.

*(**KAY** enters quickly by the French windows.* **LATIMER** *follows slowly.)*

KAY. She did. She did. Of course she did.

NEVILE. *(Angrily.)* Have you been listening?

KAY. Of course I have. And Audrey did it, I tell you. I've known she did it all the time. Don't you understand? She tried to get you hanged.

(He ignores her and turns straight to **BATTLE.***)*

NEVILE. You won't go through with it – not now?

BATTLE. *(Slowly.)* I seem to have been wrong about the motive. But there's still the money.

KAY. What money?

BATTLE. Fifty thousand pounds comes to Mrs. Audrey Strange at Lady Tressilian's death.

KAY. *(Dumbfounded.)* To Audrey? To me. The money comes to Nevile and his wife. I'm his wife. Half the money comes to me.

BATTLE. I am informed, definitely, that the money was left in trust for Nevile Strange and "his wife Audrey Strange." She gets it, not you.

> *(He signs to* **LEACH,** *who exits quickly into the house.* **KAY** *turns to* **NEVILE.***)*

KAY. But you told me – you let me think...

NEVILE. *(Mechanically.)* I thought you knew. We – I get fifty thousand. Isn't that enough?

BATTLE. Apart from all questions of motive, facts are facts. The facts point to her being guilty.

NEVILE. All the facts showed that I was guilty yesterday.

BATTLE. That's true. But are you seriously asking me to believe that there's someone who hates both of you? Someone who, if the plan failed against you, laid a second trail to Audrey Strange? Can you think of anyone who hates both you and your former wife sufficiently for that?

NEVILE. *(Crushed.)* No – no.

KAY. Of course Audrey did it. She planned it...

> *(***LEACH** *enters from the house.* **AUDREY** *follows, moving like a sleepwalker.)*

AUDREY. You wanted me, Superintendent?

BATTLE. *(Officially.)* Audrey Strange, I arrest you on the charge of murdering Camilla Tressilian on Thursday last, September the twenty-first. I must caution you that anything you say will be written down and may be used in evidence at your trial.

> *(***LEACH** *takes a notebook and pencil from his pocket, and stands waiting.* **AUDREY** *stares straight at* **NEVILE** *as though hypnotised.)*

AUDREY. So it's come at last – it's come.

> *(***NEVILE** *turns away.)*

NEVILE. Where's Treves? Don't say anything. I'm going to find Treves.

(He exits by the French windows, calling.)

Mr. Treves!

*(**AUDREY** sways. **ROYDE** rushes forward.)*

AUDREY. Oh – there's no escape – no escape. Dear Thomas, I'm so glad – it's all over – all over.

*(She recovers herself and turns to **BATTLE**.)*

I'm quite ready.

*(**LEACH** writes down Audrey's words. **BATTLE** remains impassive. The others stare at **AUDREY**, stupefied. **BATTLE** signs to **LEACH**. He takes **AUDREY** by the arm and leads her slowly out.)*

Scene II

(The same evening. The curtains are closed and the room is in darkness. **NEVILE** *stands alone. He crosses to the French windows and opens them to get some air.* **TREVES** *enters from the house.)*

TREVES. Ah, Nevile.

(He switches on the lights.)

NEVILE. *(Eagerly.)* Did you see Audrey?

TREVES. Yes, I've just left her.

NEVILE. How is she? Has she got everything she wants? I tried to see her this afternoon, but they wouldn't let me.

TREVES. She doesn't wish to see anybody at present.

NEVILE. Poor darling. She must be feeling awful. We've got to get her out of it.

TREVES. I am doing everything that's possible, Nevile.

NEVILE. The whole thing's an appalling mistake. Nobody in their right senses would ever believe that Audrey would be capable of killing anyone like that.

TREVES. *(Warningly.)* The evidence is very strong against her.

NEVILE. I don't care a damn for the evidence.

TREVES. I'm afraid the police are more practical.

NEVILE. You don't believe it, do you? You don't believe –

TREVES. I don't know what to believe. Audrey has always been an enigma.

NEVILE. Oh, nonsense! She's always been sweet and gentle.

TREVES. She has always appeared so, certainly.

NEVILE. Appeared so? She is. Audrey and – and violence of any sort just don't go together. Only a muddle-headed fool like Battle would believe otherwise.

TREVES. Battle is far from being a muddle-headed fool, Nevile. I have always found him particularly shrewd.

NEVILE. Well, he hasn't proved himself very shrewd over this. God, you don't agree with him, do you? You can't believe this utterly stupid and fantastic story that Audrey planned all this to – to get back on me for marrying Kay. It's too absurd.

TREVES. Is it? Love turns to hate very easily, you know, Nevile.

NEVILE. But she had no reason to hate me. That motive was exploded when I told them about – about Adrian.

TREVES. I must confess that that was a surprise to me. I was always under the impression that you had left Audrey.

NEVILE. I let everybody think so, of course. What else could I do? It's always so much worse for the woman. She'd have had to face the whole wretched business alone, with all the gossip and – and mud slinging. I couldn't let her do that.

TREVES. It was very generous of you, Nevile.

NEVILE. Anybody would have done the same. Besides, in a way, it was my fault.

TREVES. Why?

NEVILE. Well, I'd met Kay, you see, while we were at Cannes and I – I admit I was attracted. I flirted with her in a harmless sort of way, and Audrey got annoyed.

TREVES. You mean she was jealous?

NEVILE. Well, yes, I think so.

TREVES. If that was the case, she couldn't have been really in love with Adrian.

NEVILE. I don't think she was.

TREVES. Then she left you for Adrian in a fit of pique because she resented your – er – attentions to Kay?

NEVILE. Something like that.

TREVES. If that was the case, the original motive still holds good.

NEVILE. What do you mean?

TREVES. If Audrey was in love with you – if she only ran away with Adrian in a fit of pique, then she might still have hated you for marrying Kay.

NEVILE. *(Sharply.)* No! She never hated me. She was very understanding about the whole thing.

TREVES. Outwardly perhaps. What was she like underneath?

NEVILE. *(Quietly.)* You believe she did it, don't you? You believe she killed Camilla in that horrible way? It wasn't Audrey. I'll swear it wasn't Audrey. I know her, I tell you. I lived with her for four years – you can't do that and be mistaken in a person. But if you think she's guilty, what hope is there?

TREVES. I'll give you my candid opinion, Nevile. I don't think there is any hope. I shall brief the best possible counsel, of course, but there's very little case for the defence. Except insanity. I doubt if we'll get very far with that.

>   (**NEVILE** *buries his face in his hands. He speaks almost inaudibly.*)

NEVILE. Oh, God!

>   (**MARY** *enters from the house. She is very quiet and clearly under strain.*)

MARY. Mr. Treves!

>   *(She sees* **NEVILE***.)*

Er – there are sandwiches in the dining room when anyone wants them.

NEVILE. Sandwiches!

TREVES. *(Mildly.)* Life has to go on, Nevile.

NEVILE. Do you think she did it, Mary?

>   *(There is a definite pause.)*

MARY. No.

>   *(She takes* **NEVILE***'s hand.)*

NEVILE. Thank God somebody besides me believes in her.

>   (**KAY** *enters by the French windows.*)

KAY. Ted's just coming. He's running the car round into the drive. I came up through the garden.

NEVILE. What's Latimer coming here for? Can't he keep away for five minutes?

TREVES. I sent for him, Nevile. Kay very kindly took the message. I also asked Battle to come. I would prefer not to explain in detail. Let us say, Nevile, that I am trying out a last forlorn hope.

NEVILE. To save Audrey?

TREVES. Yes.

KAY. Can't you think of anything else but Audrey?

NEVILE. No, I can't.

(*LATIMER enters by the French windows.*)

LATIMER. I came as quickly as I could, Mr. Treves. Kay didn't say what you wanted me for, only that it was urgent.

KAY. I said what I was told to say. I haven't the faintest idea what it's all about.

MARY. We're all in the dark, Kay. As you heard, Mr. Treves is trying to help Audrey.

KAY. Audrey, Audrey, Audrey. It's always Audrey. I suppose she'll haunt us for the rest of our lives.

NEVILE. That's a beastly thing to say, Kay!

LATIMER. (*Angrily.*) Can't you see that her nerves are all in shreds?

NEVILE. So are everybody's.

(*ROYDE enters from the house.*)

ROYDE. Superintendent Battle is here. He says he's expected.

TREVES. Bring him in.

(*ROYDE beckons and BATTLE enters.*)

BATTLE. Good evening.

TREVES. Thank you for coming, Superintendent. It is good of you to spare the time.

NEVILE. (*Bitterly.*) Especially when you've got your victim.

TREVES. I don't think that kind of remark is going to get us anywhere, Nevile. Battle has only done his duty as a police officer.

NEVILE. I'm – I'm sorry, Battle.

BATTLE. That's all right, sir.

TREVES. Sit down, Battle.

BATTLE. Thank you, sir.

(He does so. There is a pause.)

TREVES. Mr. Royde said something to me the other day, Battle, that I've thought about a great deal since.

ROYDE. *(Surprised.)* I did?

TREVES. Yes, Thomas. You were talking about a detective story you were reading. You said that they all begin in the wrong place. The murder should not be the beginning of the story but the end. And, of course, you were quite right. A murder is the culmination of a lot of different circumstances, all converging at a given moment, at a given point. Rather fancifully, you called it zero hour.

ROYDE. I remember.

NEVILE. *(Impatiently.)* What's this got to do with Audrey?

TREVES. A great deal – it's zero hour now.

(There is a rather uncomfortable pause.)

MARY. But Lady Tressilian was murdered three days ago.

TREVES. It is not exactly Lady Tressilian's murder that I am talking about now. There are different kinds of murder. Superintendent Battle, when I put it to you, will you allow that all the evidence against Audrey Strange could have been faked? The weapon taken from her fender, her gloves stained with blood and hidden in the ivy outside her window. Her face powder, dusted on the inside of Nevile's dinner jacket. Hairs from her brush placed there as well?

*(**BATTLE** stirs uncomfortably.)*

BATTLE. I suppose it could have been done, but –

KAY. But she admitted she was guilty herself when you arrested her.

ROYDE. No, she didn't.

KAY. She said that she couldn't escape.

MARY. She said that she was glad it was all over.

KAY. What more do you want?

(*TREVES holds up a hand. They subside.*)

TREVES. Do you remember, Thomas, that when the Superintendent here was questioning you as to what you had heard on the night of the murder, you mentioned rats? Rats in the attic over your head?

ROYDE. Yes.

TREVES. That remark of yours interested me. I went up to the attic floor – I will admit, with no very clear idea in my head. The attic directly over your bedroom, Thomas, is used as a lumber room. It is full of what may be termed junk. Unwanted junk. There was heavy dust over everything except one thing. This.

(*He takes a long coil of thin rope from the bureau and passes it to* **BATTLE.** **BATTLE** *takes the rope. His eyebrows rise in surprise.*)

BATTLE. It's damp.

TREVES. Yes, it's still damp. No dust on it and damp. Thrown into the lumber room where someone thought it would never be noticed.

BATTLE. Are you going to tell us, sir, what it means?

(*He returns the rope to* **TREVES.***)

TREVES. It means that during the storm on the night of the murder, that rope was hanging from one of the windows of this house. Hanging from a window down to the water below. You said, Superintendent, that no one could have entered this house to commit murder from outside that night. That isn't quite true. Someone could have entered from outside if this rope was hanging ready for them to climb up from the estuary.

(**LATIMER** *shifts uncomfortably.*)

BATTLE. You mean someone came from the other side? The Easterhead side?

TREVES. Yes.

(*He turns to* **NEVILE.**)

You went over on the ten thirty-five ferry. You must have got to the Easterbead Bay Hotel at about a quarter to eleven but you weren't able to find Mr. Latimer for some time, were you?

(**LATIMER** *moves as though to speak, then stops himself.*)

NEVILE. No, that's true. I looked all around, too. He wasn't in his room – they telephoned up.

LATIMER. Actually, I was sitting out on the glass enclosed terrace with a fat, talkative body from Lancashire. (*Easily.*) She wanted to dance but I stalled her off. Too painful on the feet.

TREVES. Strange wasn't able to find you until half past eleven. Three-quarters of an hour. Plenty of time...

LATIMER. Look here, what do you mean?

NEVILE. Do you mean that he...?

(**KAY** *looks agitated. She moves to* **LATIMER.**)

TREVES. Plenty of time to strip, swim across the estuary – it's narrow just here – swarm up the rope, do what you had to do, swim back, get into your clothes and meet Nevile in the lounge of the hotel.

LATIMER. Leaving the rope hanging from the window? You're crazy – the whole thing's crazy.

(**TREVES** *gives a slight glance towards* **KAY.**)

TREVES. The same person who arranged the rope for you could have drawn it up again and put it in the attic.

LATIMER. (*Frenzied.*) You can't do this to me. You can't frame me – and don't you try. I couldn't climb up a rope all that way – and anyway, I can't swim. I tell you, I can't swim.

KAY. No, Ted can't swim. It's true, I tell you. He can't swim.

TREVES. *(Gently.)* No, you can't swim. I have ascertained that fact.

(He turns to NEVILE.*)*

But you're a very fine swimmer, aren't you, Nevile? And you're an expert climber. It would be child's play to you to swim across, climb up the rope you'd left ready, go along to Lady Tressilian's room, kill her, and go back the way you came. Plenty of time to dispose of the rope when you got back at two-thirty. You didn't see Latimer at the hotel between ten forty-five and eleven-thirty, but he didn't see you either. It cuts both ways.

*(*BATTLE *rises and stands in front of the door to the house.)*

NEVILE. I never heard such rubbish! Swim across – kill Camilla. Why ever should I do such a fantastic thing?

TREVES. Because you wanted to hang the woman who had left you for another man. She had to be punished – your ego has been swelling for a long time, nobody must dare to oppose you.

NEVILE. Is it likely I'd fake all those clues against myself?

TREVES. It's exactly what you did do – and took the precaution of ringing Lady Tressilian's bell, by pulling the wire outside her room, to make sure that Mary would see you leaving the house. Lady Tressilian didn't remember ringing that bell. You rang it.

NEVILE. What an absurd pack of lies.

*(*NEVILE *moves towards the French windows but* LEACH *appears to block his path.)*

TREVES. You murdered Lady Tressilian – but the real murder, the murder that you gloated over secretly, was the murder of Audrey Strange. You wanted her not only to die but to suffer. You wanted her to be afraid. She was afraid of you. You enjoyed the idea of her suffering, didn't you?

NEVILE. *(Thickly.)* All – a tissue of lies.

BATTLE. Is it? I've met people like you before, people with a mental kink. Your vanity was hurt when Audrey Strange left you, wasn't it? You loved her and she had the colossal impertinence to prefer another man.

(**NEVILE** *shifts uncomfortably.*)

You wanted to think of something special, something clever, something quite out of the way. The fact that it entailed the killing of a woman who had been almost a mother to you didn't worry you.

NEVILE. She shouldn't have ticked me off like a child, but it's lies – all lies. And I haven't got a mental kink.

BATTLE. Oh, yes, you have. Your wife flicked you on the raw, didn't she, when she left you? You, the wonderful Nevile Strange. You saved your pride by pretending that you'd left her – and you married another girl just to bolster up that story.

KAY. Oh.

(**KAY** *sways slightly.* **MARY** *puts her arm around her for support.*)

BATTLE. But all the time you were planning what you'd do to Audrey. Pity you didn't have the brains to carry it out better.

(**NEVILE** *almost whimpers.*)

NEVILE. It's not true.

(**BATTLE** *continues to break him down.*)

BATTLE. Audrey's been laughing at you, while you've been preening yourself and thinking how clever you were.

(*He raises his voice and calls.*)

Come in, Mrs. Strange.

(AUDREY enters from the house. NEVILE gives a strangled cry. ROYDE puts a protective arm round her.)

She's never been really under arrest, you know. We just wanted to keep her out of your crazy reach. There was no knowing what you might do if you thought your silly childish plan was going wrong.

(BENSON appears at the French windows. NEVILE looks about wildly. Trapped, he suddenly breaks down, screaming with rage.)

NEVILE. It wasn't silly. It was clever – it was clever. I thought out every detail. How was I to know that Royde knew the truth about Audrey and Adrian? Audrey and Adrian!

(He loses control and screams at AUDREY.)

How dare you prefer Adrian to me? God damn and blast your soul! You shall hang! They've got to hang you. They've got to.

(He makes a dash towards AUDREY. BATTLE quickly blocks his path. LEACH and BENSON grab NEVILE and try to restrain him. He thrashes violently.)

Leave me alone! I want her to die afraid – to die afraid! I hate her!

(AUDREY turns away, sobbing. MARY looks at NEVILE and speaks almost inaudibly.)

MARY. Oh, God!

BATTLE. Take him away, Jim.

(LEACH and BENSON lead NEVILE to the door. He suddenly becomes quite calm.)

NEVILE. You're making a great mistake, you know. I can...

(NEVILE suddenly kicks BENSON and pushes him into LEACH. Free of their grasp, he runs.

He opens the door and exits quickly into the
house.)

BATTLE. Look out! Stop him.

(**LEACH** and **BENSON** quickly recover and run
out after **NEVILE. BATTLE** follows.)

(Shouting.) After him! Don't let him get away.

(**TREVES** and **ROYDE** bring up the rear,
running after **BATTLE.** Shouting is heard off.)

ROYDE. (Offstage.) He's locked himself in the dining room!

BATTLE. (Offstage.) Break the door open!

(Heavy blows on the door are heard. **KAY**
buries her face in **LATIMER**'s shoulder and
sobs.)

KAY. Ted – oh, Ted...

(A crash of breaking glass is heard, followed
by the sound of the door breaking open.)

BATTLE. (Offstage.) Jim, you go down by the road. I'll take
the cliff path!

(**BATTLE** enters quickly from the house and
makes for the French windows.)

(Breathlessly.) He flung himself through the dining
room window. It's a sheer drop to the rocks below. I
shouldn't think there was a chance.

(**BATTLE** exits by the French windows. **BENSON**
follows immediately after him, giving three
shrill blasts on his whistle.)

KAY. (Hysterically.) I want to get away. I can't...

MARY. Why don't you take her back to the hotel with you,
Mr. Latimer?

KAY. Yes. Ted, please! Anything to get away from here.

MARY. Take her. I'll have her things packed and sent over.

LATIMER. (Gently.) Come along.

(**KAY** *exits with* **LATIMER** *by the French windows.* **MARY** *nods and exits quickly into the house.* **AUDREY** *sits heavily on the sofa and sobs. There is a slight pause, then the curtain of the bay window parts.* **NEVILE** *enters quietly over the sill. His hair is dishevelled and he has streaks of dirt on his hands and face. He wears a cruel and devilish smile as he moves silently towards* **AUDREY**. *He grabs her savagely from behind, covering her mouth with his hand.)*

NEVILE. Audrey!

(*She struggles desperately. He restrains her, speaking in a low, tense voice.*)

You didn't think I'd come back, did you? I was too clever for them, Audrey. While they were breaking open the door I flung a stool through the window and climbed out on to the stone ledge. Only a man who is used to mountain climbing could have done it – a man with strong fingers like mine.

(*She struggles again.*)

Strong fingers, Audrey – and a soft throat.

(*His fingers close round her neck.*)

They wouldn't hang you, as I wanted them to, would they? But you're going to die just the same.

(*He tightens his grip, choking her.*)

You'll never belong to anyone but me.

(**LEACH** *dashes in from the house,* **BENSON** *through the French windows. They tackle* **NEVILE**, *dragging him off* **AUDREY**. *They quickly lead him struggling through the French windows.* **AUDREY** *falls on the sofa, gasping for breath.* **ROYDE** *enters quickly from the house. He makes straight for the*

French windows, not noticing **AUDREY**. *As he passes, he catches sight of her.)*

ROYDE. I say, are you all right?

AUDREY. Am I all right? Oh, Thomas...

(**ROYDE** *takes her strongly in his arms. She sobs, broken in his embrace.)*

End of the Play

THE AGATHA CHRISTIE COLLECTION

Agatha Christie is regarded as the most successful female playwright of all time. Her illustrious dramatic career spans forty-two years, countless acclaimed original plays, several renowned novels adapted for stage, and numerous collections of thrilling one-act plays. Testament to Christie's longevity, these plays continue to engage great artists and enthral audiences today.

Since the première of her first play in 1930 the world of theatre has changed immeasurably, and so has the way plays are published and performed. Embarking upon a two-year project, Agatha Christie Limited sought to re-open Christie's distinguished body of dramatic work, looking to both original manuscripts and the most recent publications to create a "remastered" edition of each play. Each new text would contain only the words of Agatha Christie (or adaptors she personally worked with) and all extraneous materials that might come between the interpreter and the playwright would be removed, ultimately bringing the flavor and content of the texts closer to what the author would have delivered to the rehearsal room. Each new edition would then be specifically tailored to the needs and requirements of the professional twenty-first century artist.

The result is The Collection.

Whether in a classic revival or new approach, The Collection has been purposely assembled for the contemporary theatre professional. The choice and combination of plays offers something for all tastes and kinds of performance with the skill, imagination and genius of Agatha Christie's work now waiting to be explored anew in theatre.

For more information on The Collection, please visit
agathachristielimited.com/licensing/stage/browse-by-play

Lightning Source UK Ltd.
Milton Keynes UK
UKHW010047240119
336085UK00005B/558/P